ADVANCE PRAISE FOR *THE WRONG STORY*

"Greg Shupak's book is a nuanced, engaging and accessible deconstruction of the often distorted media narratives around Palestine/Israel. He compels the reader to see beyond simplistic headlines and overly rehearsed soundbites." —Rafeef Ziadah, University of London, author and performer of *We Teach Life*

"By refusing the 'both sides' narrative Greg Shupak reminds the reader of the asymmetrical relation between the colonizer and the colonized … Distortions, falsifications and omissions, the author asserts, have largely been characteristic of existing media. I highly recommend this book for media students and experts." —Nahla Abdo, Carleton University, author *of Captive Revolution*

"Shupak's *The Wrong Story* is a crisply written yet formidable analysis of some of the key tropes underlying media narratives surrounding Palestine–Israel. Neatly organized around the *New York Times'* coverage of Israel's attacks against the Gaza Strip in 2014, the book powerfully reveals the hidden histories of colonization, dispossession, and occupation." —Adam Hanieh, University of London, author *of Capitalism and Class in the Gulf Arab States*

"A powerful and insightful analysis that confronts, challenges and exposes the systematically deceptive f
glish-language mainstream media r
tinian people. Shupak's careful and p
realities that are routinely evaded by m
—Charlotte Kates, International Co
Prisoner Solidarity Network

"Gregory Shupak dismantles the mainstream English-language press' deeply problematic—and false—narrative about Palestine ... Give this book both to those interested in learning (or unlearning) about Palestine, and to those eager to learn about deconstructing the media's lies and, unfortunately, all too often the false framing of the so-called human rights organizations."
—Rania Masri, Professor

"In the tradition of Norman Finkelstein's work, Shupak uses evidence to challenge three dominant narratives presented by the mainstream media about the Israeli-Palestinian conflict. ... This book is a great teaching tool about the Israeli occupation of Palestine for university students as well as general audiences." —Angela Joya, University of Oregon

"In his judicious study of corporate media narratives on the Israel-Palestine conflict, Gregory Shupak uncovers and debunks the misleading tropes that have allowed Israel to maintain its military and expansionist policies." —Jerome Klassen, University of Massachusetts Boston, author of *Joining Empire*

"The unrelenting, decades-long pattern of biased media coverage of the Israel/Palestine conflict has had deadly consequences for the Palestinians. In *The Wrong Story*, Greg Shupak demonstrates not only how and why the media are so awful on this issue, but also what coverage of Israel/Palestine reveals about media frames and biases more generally."— Justin Podur, York University, author *of Haiti's New Dictatorship*

THE WRONG STORY

PALESTINE, ISRAEL, AND THE MEDIA

GREG SHUPAK

OR Books
New York · London

© 2018 Greg Shupak

Published by OR Books, New York and London
Visit our website at www.orbooks.com

First printing 2018

Cataloging-in-Publication data is available from the Library of Congress. A catalog record for this book is available from the British Library.

ISBN 978-1-68219-128-6 paperback
ISBN 978-1-68219-129-3 e-book

This book is set in the typeface Amalia Pro
Typeset by AarkMany Media, Chennai, India.

CONTENTS

INTRODUCTION

News media outlets tell stories. This happens at the level of individual pieces that provide accounts of real-life characters, events, and places. News outlets also construct metanarratives about issues that receive repeated coverage over an extended period. When a topic is presented in a similar fashion widely and frequently, these approaches coalesce into relatively coherent narratives through which those segments of the public that depend on news media to comprehend the world around them come to understand the subject.

This book examines three such narratives that are pervasive in coverage of Palestine-Israel. Chapter One discusses the position that "both sides" of Palestine-Israel are victims of, and at fault for, the ongoing violence to a comparable extent. Chapter Two considers the view that Palestine-Israel is largely a conflict between "extremists and moderates." The third chapter looks at news media outlets that frame Palestine-Israel in terms of Israel's supposed "right to defend itself" against Palestinian violence. To say that particular narratives are persistent is not to say that every word in every media story about Palestine-Israel rigidly conforms to one of those narratives. Nor is it to deny that outright deviations from these paradigms exist or preclude the possibility of other narratives being identified. The point is that recurring tropes spread across multiple media outlets in material published in different years about disparate events in Palestine-Israel are grounds for concluding the narratives that I identify are persistent.

In each chapter of this book, I demonstrate that the narrative under consideration is both widespread and distorted. Each one misleads, furthermore, in a manner favorable to Israel. The "both sides" narrative identifies a small portion of the injustice done to Palestinians while proportionately inflating the harm done to Israelis. This perspective, moreover, advances a false equivalency between the rights and responsibilities of the colonizers and the colonized. Framing Palestine-Israel in terms of "extremists and moderates" diagnoses the problem of ongoing violence as being a result of Palestinian terrorists and in some cases a fringe of hardline Israelis. Such a view implies that Palestinians resistant to US-Israeli prerogatives are dangerous fanatics as are Israel's settlers and far right and prescribes the solution of isolating Palestinians who are unwilling to accommodate US-Israeli designs and empowering more pliable

Palestinians. This narrative also suggests that the right wing fringes of the Israeli polity are deviations from an otherwise civilized society who can be brought under control by the majority of the country's ruling class, which is allegedly democratic and peace-seeking. The story of "Israel defending itself" supposes that the question of Palestine is unresolved because of Palestinian attacks, judges Palestinian militants' engagement in armed conflict to be unjustified and Israel's involvement to be justified, and advocates solutions characterized by Palestinian surrender and Israeli dominance.

Narratives such as these emerge when an issue is repeatedly covered using the same media frame. "To frame," according to Robert Entman, "is to select some aspects of a perceived reality and make them more salient in a communicating text, in such a way as to promote a particular problem definition, causal interpretation, moral evaluation, and/or treatment recommendation for the item described. Typically frames diagnose, evaluate, and prescribe."[1] Through these processes, the media send messages about the nature of socio-political problems, their causes, who bares responsibility for them, how conflicts can be resolved, and which parties must take which actions for that to happen. Joseph N. Cappella and Kathleen Hall Jamieson write that "news frames are those rhetorical and stylistic choices, reliably identified in news" which have the capacity to "alter the interpretations of the topics treated and are a consistent part of the news environment."[2] By taking these approaches, media outlets construct overarching stories about the subject in question.

The stories told about Palestine-Israel are as notable for what they exclude as they are for what they include. Narrative frames, as Entman points out, "are defined by what they omit as well as include, and the omissions of potential problem definitions, explanations, evaluations, and recommendations may be as critical as the inclusions in guiding the audience."[3]

The frames through which stories are presented direct audiences toward specific understandings of issues by highlighting some details at the expense of the others and emphasizing particular contexts while obscuring others. Presenting Palestine-Israel as a conflict in which "both sides" have wronged and been wronged to comparable degrees means burying such matters as, for example, the 1948 Nakba in which Palestinians were ethnically cleansed in order to create the Israeli state. When the Palestine-Israel question is described as a story about violent "extremists" who have prevented a solution from taking hold, this account necessarily leaves out the ways that peace has been undermined by the systemic economic and geo-political forces that drive Israeli colonization and the American role in enabling that colonization. A narrative that emphasizes "Israel's right to defend itself" requires leaving out the Palestinians' right to defend themselves as well as the persistent pattern of Israel initiating fighting and killing where more Palestinians are killed by Israelis by an order of magnitude.

Nothing in this book should be taken to suggest that audiences consist entirely of dupes who uncritically accept whatever the media says. People can and do think critically about the media they consume. Yet when media outlets misrepresent issues, they hamper the public's capacity to systematically understand the topics of the day. Ideally, the news media would present the public with easily accessible, comprehensive depictions of the world that people can draw on during the often short periods available to them to learn about political affairs in their daily lives. This, however, is far from the case. Viewers, readers, and listeners who approach news media with skeptical attitudes may have a general sense that they are being presented with skewed perspective. However, absent readily available and more precise information, skepticism does not necessarily translate into a clearer grasp of the issues being covered.

The stories presented in news media are not disseminated in a vacuum and it is necessary to understand that they are circulated in specific cultural contexts. According to Faiza Hirji, ruling class techniques for securing ideological hegemony "only work when they are affirming beliefs that are already held by media viewers or readers."[4] A multitude of factors shape those political views such as one's class position, gender, racial identity, educational background, or the national or cultural groups to which they belong. While news media is not the only source that influences ideology, it is undoubtedly an important source: consumption of a media text can craft the conceptual frames that will then be applied to future acts of media consumption. Similarly, Capella and Jamieson contend that: "Frames not only make the interpretations possible but they also alter the kinds of inferences made. The inferences derive from well established knowledge structures held by the audience and cued by the messages read or watched."[5]

In the West, narratives about Palestine-Israel activate the "well established knowledge structures" that exist in a broader cultural context that is colonial, imperialist, Orientalist, or some combination of these, wherein Israel is widely regarded as an outpost of Western civilization in a struggle with backward, savage Arabs. "Frames," Capella and Jamieson argue, "may be able to activate knowledge, stimulate stocks of cultural mores and values, and create contexts within which what are typically called media effects are produced." In the case of Palestine-Israel, the stories that are told register in an ideological climate that is deeply Islamophobic, anti-Arab, and permeated by fears of terror attacks.

This book pays close attention to *The New York Times'* summer 2014 editorials on Israel's Operation Protective Edge. Focusing on that newspaper is warranted because it is perhaps the most influential print media source in the United States, if not the entire English-speaking world. Because most of the media articles that I examine are from 2014, I have tried to the greatest extent possible to evaluate them with sources published before the commentary being discussed. Using this approach means that important contexts that are left out of the media narratives I consider were readily available to their authors when they wrote the articles in question. This book also looks at analysis from other publications, as well as writing on other recent events in Palestine-Israel, so as to demonstrate that the narratives I am assessing are widespread and not confined to the *New York Times* or to the summer of 2014.

By chronicling the flaws of news media narratives about Palestine-Israel, I hope that this text will contribute to undoing some of the widespread misapprehensions about the issue. My aim is for readers to see that the story of Palestine-Israel is not one of two sides who have wronged each other to comparable extents, or of a question that can be solved by isolating an extremist fringe and empowering moderates, or of an Israeli state defending itself that perhaps sometimes goes too far. I will consider this book a success to the extent that it encourages readers to reject these narratives and instead regard Palestine-Israel as what Nahla Abdo describes as a story of:

> …two asymmetrical entities; one is colonizer and oc-
> cupier and the other is colonized and occupied; one is
> a regional military superpower and the other is a large-
> ly demilitarized entity; one is independent with almost
> unlimited financial aid from the West …and the other is
> heavily dependent for its breathing, drinking and feed-
> ing, on the air, water, and land that Israel [controls]….In
> this relationship of occupier and occupied, this asym-
> metrical relation between those who order and practice
> the destruction, and those who receive its wrath, one
> cannot equate between the victim and the victimizer, let
> alone, blame the victim for the violence.[6]

CHAPTER ONE: NOT "BOTH SIDES"

The New York Times' editorials on Operation Protective Edge—Israel's assault on the Gaza Strip in the summer of 2014— demonstrate that the "both sides" narrative is commonplace and flawed. The UN[1] reports that during the hospitalities 2,251 Palestinians died, including 1,460 civilians, 556 of whom were children, while 900 were permanently disabled, 100,000 had their homes destroyed or severely damaged, and 258 schools and 78 hospitals and clinics in Gaza were damaged. 68 Israelis were killed, five of them civilians, and one of them a child.[2] In early June of that year, the two most powerful Palestinian political forces, Hamas and the Palestinian Authority (PA), reached an agreement on a national consensus government. Israel considered Hamas, which had won the most recent election in Gaza, a terrorist entity whereas the PA governed the West Bank and coordinated security there with Israel. By June 2014, Hamas' relations with key allies in Iran and Syria frayed over Hamas' reluctance to side with the Syrian government in the war in that country. In Egypt, the Hamas-allied Muslim Brotherhood was ousted in a 2013 coup through which

General Abdel Fattah el-Sisi took power. Sisi is vehemently anti-Hamas and dismantled the network of tunnels that, because of an American-Israeli-Egyptian siege on Gaza, were used to bring weapons into Gaza as well as the goods into that Hamas needed to generate tax revenues. Hamas was internationally isolated and cash-starved and it therefore agreed to a unity government that would be dominated by the PA[3] and that would recognize Israel and reject violence. However, as I explain in Chapter Three, Israel, the US and its European partners sabotaged the deal.[4] These were the political dynamics underlying Operation Protective Edge. In the sections that follow, I will discuss other important events in the lead up to the war such as the killings and abductions of Palestinian and Israeli youth, Israeli airstrikes on Gaza, and rocket fire into Israel by Hamas and other Palestinian factions.

THE *TIMES* ASSIGNS BLAME

As I have noted, the "both sides" paradigm has two main facets. It presents Palestine-Israel as a story of two sides deserving more or less equal portions of blame for the absence of peace and of Israelis and Palestinians experiencing comparable pain as a result. I will begin this section by looking at how the first of these is present in the *Times*' editorial coverage of Protective Edge.

The first *Times* editorial on Protective Edge was on July 8th, 2014.[5] The article discusses the kidnapping and killing of three Israeli teenagers by Palestinians in the West Bank and the subsequent kidnapping and killing of a Palestinian teenager by Israelis. The editors write that these incidents could lead to a full-blown war and that "It is the responsibility of leaders on both sides" to stop that from happening. The editors then claim that the "hostilities and recriminations began with the kidnapping and murder" of the three Israeli teenagers. The claim that this round of antagonisms "began" with the abduction of the Israeli youth is dubious even if one sets aside the broader context of Israeli colonialism in which these events played out. The three Israelis were kidnapped on June 12th, whereas on May 15th the Israeli military shot and killed two unarmed Palestinian teenagers at a demonstration organized to both express solidarity with Palestinian prisoners on a hunger strike and to commemorate Nakba Day, which is when Palestinians mark the mass dispossession of, and displacement from, their homeland that took place during the creation of the state of Israel.[6] If Operation Protective Edge was partially a consequence of the mutual killings of teenagers, it is only possible to say that these episodes "began" with the deaths of the Israeli youth if the killing of the Palestinian teens less than a month earlier is overlooked. The erasure of these dead Palestinian youth is most dramatic in the editorial's first sentence, which is written as though the May 15th victims did not exist: "In the space of a few weeks, the brutal killings of four teenagers—one Palestinian and three Israelis—have inflamed tensions in Israel and the occupied territories." Further underscoring this point is that the killings of those two Palestinian youth brought the total of Palestinian children killed by Israeli forces in 2014 to four, according to the UN-affiliated Defense for Children International-Palestine.[7]

Blame for the violence leading up to and during Protective Edge is addressed in July 8th, July 19th[8], and August 7th[9] editorials. Yet none of them note that Israel started the violence. The July 19th editorial lays most of the blame on Hamas. It says that Israel sent ground forces into Gaza "to keep Hamas from pummeling Israeli cities with rockets and carrying out terrorist attacks via underground tunnel." In other words, the paper claims that Israel's land incursion was a response to Hamas' violence even though Israel provoked the rocket fire and even though there is a paucity of evidence that the tunnels were being used to attack Israeli civilians. The editors say that Hamas leaders "deserve condemnation" for allegedly inviting Israeli fire on Palestinian civilians while the harshest criticism that the paper offers of Israeli leadership is to say that military action is "not a long-term solution" and that Obama was right to "express concern" about "the risks of further escalation and the loss of more innocent life." Meanwhile, the August 7th editorial says that "both sides" are worthy of blame for the carnage. Yet the first rockets fired from Gaza were on June 13th, whereas Israeli airstrikes began on June 11th [10] when the Israeli Air Force targeted an alleged militant riding a motorcycle together with a ten-year old child. The motorcyclist was killed instantly. The child sustained serious injuries and died three days later. Two civilian bystanders were also injured.[11] Omitting this essential piece of information benefits the Israeli state by contriving the Palestinians' responsibility for the bloodshed while hiding Israel's. In these two editorials, the "both sides" narrative operates by selecting starting points for Protective Edge that favor Israel because this version of events rationalizes the destruction inflicted by Israel on Gaza, which as I show below was far greater than the destruction Palestinian armed groups caused in Israel. The story of Protective Edge is told in a way that speciously implies that Israel is at fault for going too far at times but that Palestinians are at fault for starting the fighting and that therefore both sides are in the wrong. This narrative depends on concealing Israel's killing of the two Palestinian teenagers on May 15th and Israel's June 11th airstrikes, to say nothing of the larger historical and contemporary picture discussed below.

A more accurate accounting of what happened would be that the Israeli state had started a war against a population made up mostly of people that it made refugees.[12] This condition is part of a colonizing process that began well before the creation of the state of Israel and can be traced back to the beginning of the 20th century. The long-running siege of Gaza is also a crucial context. In 2005, Israel dismantled its settlements in Gaza, evacuated their residents, and withdrew its military forces from inside of the territory. Israel, however, maintained effective control over its borders with Gaza and over Gaza's airspace and territorial waters. In short, Israel still occupies Gaza.[13] When Hamas won the 2006 Palestinian election, Israel imposed a blockade on Gaza and tightened it in 2007 when Hamas won control of the territory in a struggle with the PA. The UN suggested in 2012 that without "sustained and effective remedial action and an enabling political environment," Gaza might not be "liveable" by 2020.[14] A January 2014 report from the Israeli human rights group B'Tselem notes that the siege "has economically paralyzed the Strip—90 percent of the factories and thousands of businesses have closed down," and that the siege has "led to a sharp drop in the availability of basic items, including food and medicines."[15]

The blockade was one of the central concerns of the Palestinians during Protective Edge.[16] In a 2012 ceasefire that was reached to end Israel's operation Pillar of Defense, Israel agreed to "Opening the crossings and facilitating the movements of people and transfer of goods and refraining from restricting residents' free movements," which would have meant lifting or significantly easing of the siege. Israel, however, did not follow through on this agreement and that was a crucial factor behind the 2014 violence.[17] Early in Protective Edge, Hamas and other Palestinian armed groups rejected a ceasefire, which they had no part in crafting and which was put forth by their enemies in Israel and Egypt, largely because it offered no assurances that the siege would be lifted.[18] Yet of the five *Times* editorials written during and immediately before Operation Protective Edge, the blockade of Gaza is only mentioned in the August 7th article. This lack of attention is necessary for the "both sides" narrative to hold: since only "one side" was besieging the other, the mere existence of a siege is itself enough to puncture the "both sides" narrative. Keeping to the "both sides" framework deprives readers of a context that is central to understanding Protective Edge. Obscuring the importance of the siege to Palestinians distorts the narrative of Protective Edge in Israel's favor. Paying so little attention to the blockade removes a major grievance of the Palestinians, thereby hiding a key reason for their willingness to fight while also consigning to the background what both the Palestinians and many respected international organizations see as a major Israeli wrong.

THE *TIMES* ON THE PAIN OF OPERATION PROTECTIVE EDGE

Editorials in *The New York Times* repeatedly presented Operation Protective Edge as a war in which both Israelis and Palestinians were harmed to comparable degrees. The *Times*' July 19th editorial tells readers in the second sentence that "The tragedy is that innocent civilians on both sides of the border are paying the price, once again."[19] Having this phrase at the outset establishes "both sides" as the article's operative frame. The frame is reinforced by the structure of the article, which primarily consists of shifting between the sins the paper attributes to Hamas and to the Israeli government as well as between the difficulties faced by civilians in Gaza and in Israel. This framing arguably mitigates the casualty figures noted in the editorial, which reveal that one side is paying a much steeper price: "Only two Israelis have died" whereas there were "260 Palestinians killed, three-quarters were civilians, including more than 50 children." The paper deviates somewhat from its practices in other Protective Edge editorials by providing concrete examples of Israeli attacks on Palestinians: "Innocent Palestinians are being killed and brutalized: four Palestinians boys playing on a beach; four children playing on a rooftop; a rehabilitation hospital, all destroyed by Israeli firepower." These deaths, however, are subsumed within the "both sides" narrative as they follow the paper's account of how "Well over 1,000 rockets have fallen on Israel since July 8, and they have reached farther than ever, threatening Tel Aviv and beyond" and of how "Israeli citizens are running for cover from incoming rockets." The equivalency is false: Palestinians were "threatened" by and "running for cover" from Israeli weaponry to a far more dramatic extent than were Israelis from Palestinians. This is clear given that Israeli deaths occurred at 1/180th the rate they did in Gaza and given that 22,900 Gaza residents had been displaced by Protective Edge at that point and were being hosted at United Nations Relief and Works Agencies (UNRWA) schools while Israelis did not face displacement on a similar scale.[20]

In its July 25th editorial, the *Times'* writes that "the war is terrorizing innocent people on both sides of the [Israel-Gaza] border."[21] A day before the editorial was published, the UN reported that two Israeli civilians had died since Protective Edge began compared to a minimum of 578 Palestinian civilians, including 185 children.[22] The report notes that the Israeli military declared 44% of Gaza a "no-go zone," which together with "unremitting hostilities" was "restricting the movement and security of Palestinian civilians and the ability of humanitarian actors to carry out even the most basic life-saving activities, adding to the growing despair" of Gaza residents.[23] Considering the gaps in these casualty figures, considering that 44% of Israel was not declared a "no-go zone" and that Israelis were not being denied access to life-saving activities, significant features of the situation are obscured when readers are merely told that "innocent people on both sides" are being terrorized. Moreover, less than a week before this editorial was published, "intense Israeli bombardment of [the Gaza City neighbourhood] Shuja'iyyeh killed more than 60 people, including at least 17 children,"[24] according to Amnesty International, and Doctors Without Borders says there were hundreds of civilians wounded in the neighborhood.[25]

Also relevant is a report released one day prior to the *Times*' editorial from The Palestine Centre for Human Rights (PRCHR), a group that holds Special Consultative Status with the Economic and Social Council (ECOSOC) of the United Nations. PCHR says that on July 23rd and 24th, Israeli warplanes carried out 50 airstrikes "targeting houses, civilians, agricultural plots" in the Gaza town of Khan Yunis, killing 39 Palestinians, 5 of whom were children, and wounding a further 165 Palestinians, 42 of them children.[26] Meanwhile, Israeli forces prevented medical crews and ambulances from reaching the victims.[27] When Israeli forces moved into Khuza'a, a village in the southeast of the Gaza Strip, they "fired bullets and artillery shells at hundreds of Palestinian civilians who attempted to leave the village" and fired at dozens of Palestinian civilians holding up white flags, forcing them back to their homes.[28] A UN[29] report issued July 23rd says that, according to preliminary information, Israeli forces killed at least 20 persons in Khuza'a. No mass violence against civilians on the scale that took place in Shuja'iyyeh, Khan Yunis, and Khuza'a occurred in Israel so it is a distorted picture that simply describes "terrorizing innocent people on both sides" without even mentioning that Israel had inflicted mass killings and injuries on Palestinians in three separate incidents within the week.

Furthermore, in Gaza at the time, 149,000 people were displaced, 167,000 were in need of emergency food assistance, 18 health facilities were damaged or destroyed, and 1.2 million of Gaza's 1.8 inhabitants had no or very limited access to water or sanitation services.[30] Remotely comparable conditions did not exist in Israel so it's misleading to speak of undifferentiated, terrorized innocent civilians on both sides. Using the "both sides" narrative papers over these differences between the Palestinians' experience of the fighting and that of the Israelis' experience. This narrative erases what the reports from Amnesty, the PCHR, and the UN make clear: far more Palestinians than Israelis were suffering. In these respects, the *Times* offers a version of events that misrepresents what was happening in Israel's favor.

The August 7th editorial, like the one from July 25th, emphasizes the feelings of terror associated with the violence. The article notes that at that point 1,800 mostly civilian Palestinians had died, including 408 children, compared to 67 Israelis. After the editorial gives an overview of the damage done in Gaza, it says that "There are important but less tangible costs: the way ordinary Israelis have had to live in fear of rocket attacks." The fear Israelis experienced is presented as a counterweight to the discrepancy in the casualty toll. The suggestion that there is a balance between the harm done to Israelis and that which was done to Palestinians in Gaza rests on the notion that mass Israeli fear is comparable to mass Palestinian death and injury. The premise that terror is as undesirable as death is itself questionable but the equation entirely falls apart when one considers that, while casualties in the thousands were unique to the Palestinian experience of Protective Edge, living in fear was not unique to the Israeli experience. For example, in Rafah, a Palestinian city and refugee camp in southern Gaza, Israel killed 45 Palestinians between August 1st and August 3rd, including 40 civilians and 10 children, wounding another 50 civilians, 21 of them children.[31] Inhabitants of Rafah, therefore, had ample reason to "live in fear."

In these ways, the "both sides" narrative favors the Israeli government by downplaying the harm Israel has inflicted on Palestinians and inflating the harm done to Israeli civilians.

BEYOND THE *TIMES*

The New York Times' editorial board is far from the only purveyor of the "both sides" narrative. In the lead up to Protective Edge, *The Guardian*'s editors blame "both sides' political impotence" for enabling the environment in which the June and July 2014 murders of the Israeli and Palestinian teenagers took place.[32] Another editorial in that paper describes Protective Edge as "cruel beyond words on civilians" as if Israeli and Palestinian civilians experience similar degrees of cruelty or are similarly blameworthy for the war. In the same paper, Jonathan Freedland describes a "perverse landscape in which both Israelis and Palestinians find themselves. They are led by men who hear their fear and fury—and whose every action digs both peoples deeper into despair."[33] Michael Cohen, in another *Guardian* article, refers to "the tragic loss of life in Gaza and Israel" as though these were comparable in scale and as though responsibility for them were equivalent. He goes on to write of the need to "save both sides from themselves" and laments that "both Israelis and Palestinians are more interested in doing what they believe is in their narrow interests."[34]

In *The Daily Beast*, Sally Kohn writes[35] "I hate Hamas rockets being fired toward Israel as much as I hate Israeli missiles being fired at Gaza" and "One side's wrongs don't make the other side's actions any more right." While Kohn does concede that the greatest destruction during Protective Edge comes from "the far more powerful and capable Israeli military," she does so in the context of an article built around defending her position "against Hamas *and* [in] support [of] the state of Israel while simultan-eously critiquing Israel's attacks on civilians in Gaza." Moreover, James Bloodworth says in *The Independent* that "The loss of life in Gaza and the Hamas rocketing of Israel is certainly regrettable" without differentiating between the magnitude of or responsib-ility for these.[36] He also writes that "There really is something to be said for both sides . . . in the sense that both sides both have legitimate grievances." Will Gore, Deputy Managing Editor of *The Independent*, puts forth the following argument: "That *The Independent* is regarded by some on either side as favouring the other is suggestive of a balanced approach."[37]

Much of the commentary on Protective Edge uses the "both sides" narrative to describe not only the specific events of the summer of 2014 but also the Palestine-Israel question more gen-erally. For example, in the *Times*' July 8th 2014 editorial on the killings of Palestinian youth by Israelis and Israeli youth by Pales-tinians, the editors write that the climate around the killings "once again threaten[s] both peoples."[38] This remark suggests that the long-term story of Palestine-Israel has been one where both sides are in jeopardy to a similar extent. Comments like these fail to differentiate between the degrees of threat to which Israelis and Palestinians have been subjected and between the actual damage inflicted by enacting such threats. Dean Obeidallah writes in *The Daily Beast* that "Too often, people view [Palestine-Israel] as a zero sum game where even the slightest acknowledgment that the other side is suffering is an attack upon their own side."[39] He urges readers to "Stop with the knee jerk, blind defense of your own side—regardless of which that may be. Instead, if the people you support are committing acts inconsistent with your own sense of morality, then you should speak out. Maybe, just maybe, this approach will yield common ground that can be the foundation to build a bridge to peace."

Similarly, in a *Huffington Post* article published during Protective Edge and shared 56,000 times on social media, Ali A. Rizvi claims that the outstanding questions in Palestine-Israel "will never be resolved unless people stop choosing sides." He then argues that "you really don't have to choose between being "pro-Israel" or "pro-Palestine." If you support secularism, democracy, and a two-state solution — and you oppose Hamas, settlement expansion, and the occupation — you can be both."[40] H.A Goodman, also writing for *Huffington Post*, contends that "To blame one side without looking at the other is not only irresponsible, but borders on an overt attempt at circumventing the facts" and that "Gaza's occupation is legitimized by extremists on both sides." Goodman goes on to write that "The arguments beginning with "He started it" don't work anymore, especially since both Hamas and Israel have thrown moral and acceptable standards of behavior out the window."[41] When Palestine-Israel is discussed in such a manner, Lisa Taraki writes, "the dynamics arising out of the Israeli colonial project are easily viewed as a conflict or dispute between two warring sides, each of which may have legitimate and valid claims."[42] Presenting the story in this fashion inhibits readers' capacity to accurately understand how Israelis and Palestinians came to be where they are, which factors have been central to the absence of peace, whether the goal is peace in any form or peace with justice, which grievances need to be addressed, whose conduct needs to change and in which ways, and thus which policies the public should advocate for in order to achieve a peace that includes liberation for Palestinians.

ETHNIC CLEANSING

The "both sides" narrative obscures the larger contexts in which particular events in Palestine-Israel take place. Because the state of Israel is not yet 70 years old, and because it has been barely more than 100 years since the future of Palestine became a burning international question, these histories' inaugural events continue to directly shape the lives of people in or originating from the region as well as its contemporary politics and therefore must be part of any media narrative if it is to accurately inform readers. This history, however, is papered over when the story of Palestine-Israel is presented as one in which both sides have inflicted similar amounts of pain on each other. Developments in the earliest moments of the lead-up to the creation of the state of Israel demonstrate that the "both sides" narrative is erroneous.

In 1917, the British Foreign Secretary Arthur James Balfour promised to create in Palestine a "national home" for the Jewish people as the Zionist movement had hoped. Zionism has had multiple currents but the dominant strand of political Zionism in the years leading up to the creation of the state of Israel was that which, in Ilan Pappe's words, sought an "exclusively Jewish presence in Palestine" that was both "a safe haven for Jews from persecution and a cradle for a new Jewish nationalism."[43] At the end of World War One, Britain occupied Palestine, which had been part of the defeated Ottoman Empire. The League of Nations created a legal mandate for the British presence in Palestine and included the entire text of the Balfour Declaration. The declaration, Ibrahim Abu-Lughod explains, undermines the Palestinians' right to self-determination by denying the Palestinian and Arab identity of the affected people by failing to reference

"either a national or cultural designation of Palestine's population whose civil and religious rights were to be protected by its
terms; on the other hand the Declaration was very specific about
the Jewish people."[44] The League of Nations Mandate said Britain had a responsibility to help Jewish people in Palestine create
national institutions, a task that included Jewish settlement. At
the time, the population of Palestine was 10% Jewish and 90%
Arab but, as Rashid Khalidi points out, not one of the Mandate's
28 articles "related to the Palestinian people per se: they were
variously and vaguely defined as a 'section of the population,'
'natives,' or 'peoples and communities.' As far as Great Britain
and the League of Nations were concerned, they were definitely
not a people."[45]

The Zionist movement created a Palestine Foundation Fund
to organize Jewish immigration and colonization and founded
the Palestine Land Development Company as an agency of the
Jewish National Fund (JNF), which in 1901 was born from the
Jewish Colonial Trust to buy land and hold it in trust exclusively
for "the Jewish people"; non-Jewish people cannot own land the
JNF controls, a policy that continues to the present day.[46] During
the 1920s, the Palestinians made up 80-90% of the population
while the Jewish inhabitants of the land accounted for 10%-20%,
yet Britain attempted to put in place a political structure based
on parity between the two groups in contrast to the democratic

principle of majoritarian politics that Britain paid lip service to in the other Arab states where it had influence.[47] Initially, the Palestinians opposed the proposal but then changed course in view of the growing number of Jewish settlements. The Zionists switched positions in the opposite direction.[48] Britain's failure to implement their promise of parity led to the Palestinians' 1929 uprising. Britain's continued alliance with the Zionists precipitated the Palestinians' 1936-1939 popular uprising, which the British subdued with "ruthless attacks on the Palestinian countryside."[49] The Palestinian leadership was exiled, the paramilitary units it used against the Mandatory forces were broken up, and many villagers were arrested, wounded, or killed, all of which made it easier for the Zionists to take the Palestinian countryside between 1947 and 1949.[50]

On November 29th 1947, the United Nations General Assembly passed Resolution 181, which is also known as the Partition Resolution. The resolution divided Palestine, creating one Arab state and one larger Jewish state. The Jewish state was granted the most fertile land[51] and the resolution said that the City of Jerusalem would be under international control and administered by the UN. The Partition Resolution did not reflect the territory's ethnic composition. Jewish people owned only 5.8% of the land, accounted for at most one third of the overall population, and inhabited less than 25% of the countryside while most of the cultivated land was held by the indigenous Palestinian majority. If the UN had created a Jewish state out of the territory on which Jewish people were living, the Jewish state would have been on 10% of Palestine or less. Instead the UN allotted the Zionists control over territory that included 499,000 Jewish people and 430,000 Palestinians and the UN allotted the Palestinians control over territory that included 818,000 Palestinians and 10,000 Jews.[52] Zionist leaders accepted the partition plan but their Palestinian counterparts and Arabs elsewhere in the region rejected it, suggesting instead that Palestine remain a unitary state and that negotiations over the future of Palestine continue.[53]

That only one side in Palestine-Israel ethnically cleansed the other demonstrates the folly of presenting Palestine-Israel as a story of two sides who have inflicted similar degrees of harm on each other and who are equally responsible for decades of violence. Through a campaign of mass violence, Zionist forces drove 750,000-800,000 Palestinians, or more than half of the Palestinian population, out of Palestine and destroyed half of their villages and towns. 531 villages were destroyed and eleven urban neighborhoods were emptied of their inhabitants.[54] Such acts were carried out by the Hagana, the Zionist's quasi-regular military force that included a commando unit called Palmach, in co-ordination with the Zionist splinter groups the Irgun and Lehi (whom the British called the Stern Gang).[55] The morning after the UN adopted the Partition Resolution, the Irgun and Hagana terrorized the 75,000 Palestinians in Haifa by setting off car bombs, covering the streets in fuel and explosives then lighting them on fire and machine-gunning Palestinians when they came out of their homes to extinguish the blazes.[56] On December 31st, Zionist forces killed more than 60 Palestinians in the village of Balad al-Shaykh and expelled the residents of Wadi Rushmiyya, an Arab neighbourhood in Haifa, blowing up their houses.[57] In March 1948, Zionist leaders began to implement Plan Dalet, a "blueprint for the expulsion of as many Palestinians as possible."[58]

Enacting this plan entailed carrying out acts of mass violence in many Palestinian towns and urban centers. The Zionist forces Irqun, Lehi, and the Hagana took the Palestinian town of Deir Yasin in April and massacred between 254 and 350 Palestinians, 75 of them children.[59] On May 14th, Israel declared itself a state. The next day Iraq, Egypt, Syria, and Tranjordan launched a joint military intervention with the support of smaller contingents from Lebanon, Saudi Arabia, Yemen, and the volunteer Arab Liberation Army. The Arab states did not stop the ethnic cleansing of Palestine. More than 60,000 Palestinians were expelled from the towns Lydda and Ramle in July with the direct involvement of senior Zionist leaders such as Yigal Allon, Moshe Dayan, Yitzhak Rabin, and David Ben-Gurion, Israel's first Prime minister.[60] At the end of October, the Israeli army massacred between 80 and

100 unarmed Palestinians, some of them children, in al-Dawayma after Israel already had control over the town and after Israel had already won the broader war. Civilian victims were thrown into pits, women were raped, houses where the elderly were locked inside were blown up.[61] Palestinians were expelled from the Galilee in a series of massacres that same month: the diary of Yosef Nahmani, director of the JNF in the Galilee, includes accounts he received of rape, and of 50-60 peasants being tied up, shot and buried in a pit in Safsaf. Nahmani recounts Israeli soldiers being greeted with food and white flags in Eilabun and Farradiya and then killing 30 people and leading the rest out of the town and toward Lebanon.[62] After Israel became a state in May 1948, it passed a series of laws giving the JNF dominion over massive tracts of Arab land "whose proprietors had become refugees, and were pronounced 'absentee landlords' in order to prevent their return under any circumstance."[63] By the end of the 1948 war, Israel had control over 78% of what had been Palestine.[64] Gaza was in the Egyptian domain while Jordan was in possession of the West Bank and East Jerusalem. Presenting Palestine-Israel as a story of parallel misdeeds and hardships obfuscates the systemic dispossessions and massacres of one side by the other, a relationship which continues to impact present day events.

It is not both sides in Palestine-Israel who are keeping millions of refugees from returning to their homes. In January 2014,

UNRWA reported having 5,030,049 registered Palestinian refugees.[65] In its biennial survey, BADIL Resource Center for Palestinian Residency and Refugee Rights, a Palestinian NGO that has special consultative status with the UN's Economic and Social Council, says that at the end of 2011 there were 7.4 million Palestinian refugees: 4.8 million registered refugees from the 1948 ethnic cleansing and another 1 million from that year who are unregistered; more than 1 million refugees from Israel's 1967 occupation of the West Bank, Gaza, and East Jerusalem; and 519,000 internally displaced persons on either sides of the Green Line, the demarcation between the state of Israel and East Jerusalem, the West Bank, the Gaza Strip, the Golan Heights, and the Sinai Peninsula, which was established in 1949 after the previous year's war.[66] While Israel's Law of Return allows anyone who the state deems Jewish to become a citizen of Israel, Israel refuses to allow Palestinian refugees to return to their homes though their right to do so is enshrined under UN Resolution 194. Media coverage suggesting that Israelis and Palestinians have wronged each other to similar extents ignores that it is only one side that made millions of people refugees and that is responsible for them continuing to have that status. Israel's abrogation of the right of Palestinian refugees to return directly impinges upon current events. Palestinians, if not always their leaders, insist on their right to return and so Israeli denial of that legally protected right is a key reason that peace eludes the peoples of Palestine-Israel and that the conditions necessary for events like Protective Edge continue. Eliding the refugee issue by subsuming it in a "both sides" framework conceals a major grievance that Palestinians have, one with a basis in international law. This narrative makes the Palestinian case appear weaker than it is and serves Israel by glossing over an injustice that the state has done, and continues to do, to the Palestinians by preventing the refugees from returning.

OCCUPATION, WAR, AND APARTHEID

Only one side in Palestine-Israel has militarily occupied the other for the last 50 years. In the 1950s, the Israeli army developed plans to occupy the West Bank.[67] Syria appeared to be facing a serious threat from Israel in the spring of 1967, so the Egyptian government, which was jostling for regional influence with Saudi Arabia, supported its Syrian ally by ratcheting up its military posture toward Israel.[68] Israel then surprised the Egyptian-Syrian-Jordanian military alliance with a June 1967 attack that ended with Israel, thanks to the superior weapons it received from Western states, in control of the West Bank, the Gaza Strip, Egypt's Sinai Peninsula, and Syria's Golan Heights.[69] In November of that year, the UN passed Resolution 242 calling on Israel to withdraw from those territories. Egypt and Syria undertook a war in October 1973 with the limited aim of liberating the territory Israel had occupied since 1967 but did not succeed.[70] The Sinai is the only territory where Israel has surrendered control. Israel gave the Sinai back to Egypt in a 1979 bilateral accord that the US brokered. An account of Palestine-Israel that reduces what has happened, and continues to happen, to a conflict between two sides is facile in that one side has militarily occupied the other for fifty years.

During that half century occupation, only one side has subjected the other to dispossession, discrimination, and mass violence. Israel's illegal separation wall cuts Palestinians off from their own land, which they can access only by passing through gates that Israel controls and that require permits issued by the military that are hard to secure.[71] At many locations, Israel has erected a system through which it controls when and where Palestinians can move—often abusing them in the process. As of 2013, Israel had over 500 checkpoints and separation barriers in the West Bank that, according to Amnesty International, limit Palestinians' access to medical care, water, and farmland.[72] These checkpoints and barriers result in lengthy delays[73] that amount to a restriction to Palestinians' free movement. Richard Falk, writing as a UN Special Rapporteur, notes that "among the salient apartheid features of the Israeli occupation" are "discriminatory arrangements for movement in the West Bank and to and from Jerusalem," such as "extensive burdening of Palestinian movement, including checkpoints applying differential limitations on Palestinians and on Israeli settlers, and onerous permit and identification requirements imposed only on Palestinians."[74] By contrast, Israelis who are illegally settled on the West Bank are allowed easy passage through the checkpoints or are allowed to travel on roads that have no checkpoints.[75] These Israeli-only highways fragment the Occupied Palestinian Territory (OPT) into tiny cantons. Palestinians require permits, which are difficult to obtain, to move from one city in the OPT to another.[76] John Dugard, a UN Special Rapporteur for human rights in the Palestinian territories, notes that the conduct of Israeli soldiers at the checkpoints is "often rough. A person may be refused passage through a checkpoint for arguing with a soldier or explaining his documents. The principle of legality, requiring a law to be clear, consistent, and published in advance, is completely unknown and disregarded at the checkpoints. Instead an arbitrary and capricious regime prevails."[77] He goes on to write that in apartheid South Africa there was "a similar system designed to restrict the free movement of blacks—the notorious 'pass laws.'"[78] Since Palestinians do not control when and where Israelis can move, and do not require that they have Palestinian authorization to do so, the military checkpoints and permit system are other aspects of the story of Palestine that are lost when it is reduced to one of "both parties" suffering and harming each other.

Only one side in Palestine-Israel, furthermore, controls the quality and quantity of the other's water. In Gaza, Israel's siege constrains the ability of Palestinians to develop a functioning water system while the import restrictions Israel enforces have, according to a 2013 UN report, "impeded the expansion and upgrading of Gaza's sewage infrastructure" so that almost 90 million liters of untreated or only partially treated sewage are discharged into the sea every day, which "poses a serious health hazard." Gaza's Coastal Municipalities Water Utility, a government utility company responsible for managing water, is hampered by Israel's limitations on the import of goods that make repairing the sewage system and water supply network difficult.[79] A 2006 airstrike on six transformers at the Gaza Power Plant, as well as Israel's restrictions on the import of spare parts, equipment, and fuel, are part of why Gaza has an insufficient supply of electricity and fuel to operate water pumps and wells, which reduces the availability of running water in most Gaza households.[80] During Operation Cast Lead, Israel's 2008-2009 assault on Gaza, water supplies and wastewater systems were affected by damage to water wells and drinking water pipes and there was an increase in pollution discharged into the Mediterranean and into the groundwater, none of which happened in Israel.[81] For Gaza's agriculture to fare well, it requires water in sufficient quantity and quality[82] so a lack of either of these is also a threat to the Palestinians' economy and their ability to eat.

Water on the West Bank is primarily under Israeli control. The Oslo accords grant Israel an unlimited supply of water and cap the amount to which Palestinians have access. In practice, Palestinians receive only 75% of their quota.[83] Furthermore, the more than 500,000 illegal Israeli settlers consume approximately six times the amount of water used by the Palestinian population of almost 2.6 million, a gap that becomes even larger when the water used for agriculture is taken into account.[84] Palestinians have had to deal with water shutoffs for days and sometimes weeks at a time,[85] a condition that does not prevail in Israel.

Furthermore, it is not both sides who torture and hold thousands of each other prisoner. In May 2014, on the eve of Protective Edge, Israel held 192 Palestinians in administrative detention.[86] This practice involves Israel jailing Palestinians for renewable periods of up to six months on the basis of secret evidence and without charges or trials. By July of 2014, during Protective Edge, the number of Palestinians that Israel was holding in administrative detention had risen to 446[87] and, at the time of writing, the total is 536.[88] The UN's Commission on Human Rights has called on Israel to stop using administrative detention.[89] Similarly, the Israeli NGO B'tselem notes "the serious injury to due-process rights inherent in this measure." The group goes on to say that:

> Israel's use of administrative detention blatantly violates the restrictions of international law. Israel carries it out in a highly classified manner that denies detainees the possibility of mounting a proper defense… Over the years, Israel has placed thousands of Palestinians in administrative detention[90] for prolonged periods of time, without trying them, without informing them of the charges against them, and without allowing them or their counsel to examine the evidence. In this way, the military judicial system ignores the right to freedom and due process, the right of defendants to state their case, and the presumption of innocence, all of which are protections clearly enshrined in both Israeli and international law.

As Protective Edge was about to begin, moreover, Israel held 5,271 Palestinian political prisoners.[91]

Israeli law explicitly discriminates against Palestinians from the occupied territories. They are prosecuted in military courts, whereas Israelis who have illegally settled those same territories have the advantage of being tried under a civilian legal system.

Under this arrangement, Israeli setters accused of crimes have greater legal rights than Palestinians in the same position. Compared to the Israelis, Palestinians processed in the military courts can be held longer before being brought before a judge, have more constraints on their right to meet with an attorney, are granted fewer protections at trial, face harsher punishments, and have less of a chance of being released before their sentence is complete.[92]

Israel also routinely tortures Palestinians. A report jointly written by Palestinian and Israeli NGOs finds that "Israeli perpetrators of human rights violations against Palestinian prisoners and detainees in custody continue to enjoy impunity due to a lack of domestic legislation prohibiting torture and a lack of proper mechanisms of complaints, documentation, investigation and prosecution."[93] Even children are subject so such practices. The UN's Committee on the Rights of the Child reports that Palestinian children are "often" subject "to acts of torture, are interrogated in Hebrew, a language they do not understand, and sign confessions in Hebrew in order to be released."[94] Given that there is no Palestinian legal system in which Israelis are persecuted, the institutional, widespread discrimination and maltreatment that Palestinians face in the Israeli judicial system is rendered invisible in news media narratives that describe a conflict in which "both sides" mutually inflict injustices on each other.

Though I have thus far concentrated on Palestinians living in the occupied territories, Palestinians living inside of the

Green Line as citizens of Israel are by no means exempt from Israeli mistreatment. Adalah, a human rights organization based in Israel, has a database of more than fifty laws that discriminate against Palestinian citizens of Israel. These include the 1953 Jewish National Fund Law, which grants the JNF governmental authority and financial advantages in purchasing land even as the JNF is an organization that explicitly discriminates against Palestinians by purchasing land for exclusively Jewish use.[95] Palestinians can be stripped of their citizenship if they are accused of participating in a violent act but no such punishment exists for the Jewish citizens of Israel.[96] The 2003 Ban on Family Unification bars, with rare exceptions, Israeli citizens who are married to Palestinians from the OPT or residents of Iran, Lebanon, Iraq, or Syria from living together in Israel and "thousands of Palestinian families have been affected by the law, forced to split apart, move abroad or live in Israel in fear of constant deportation."[97] The Nakba Law, adopted in 2011, authorizes the Finance Minister to reduce state support for an institution if it rejects the existence of Israel as a "Jewish and democratic state" or commemorates the Nakba, as Palestinians do every year on the anniversary of Israel's founding.[98] In 2011, Israel passed the Anti-Boycott Law, which prohibits the public promotion of academic, economic, or cultural boycott by Israeli citizens and organizations against Israeli institutions or illegal Israeli settlements in the West Bank[99] thereby interfering with the rights of Palestinian citizens of Israel—or any other citizens of the country—to protest against their own mistreatment or that of Palestinians living outside of Israel. It also prohibits a person who calls for boycott from participating in any public tender. Palestinian citizens of Israel are also discriminated against in the provision of state resources. In 2015, Arab towns in Israel received just 4.6% of new housing units and just 2.5% of reduced-cost housing units despite Palestinians accounting for 20% of the population and despite the housing crisis facing this group.[100] Moreover, the Association for Civil Rights in Israel (ACRI) says that "Arab citizens of Israel face entrenched discrimination in all fields of life" and that "There are glaring socioeconomic differences between Jewish and Arab population groups, particularly with regard to land, urban planning, housing, infrastructure, economic development, and education. Over half of the poor families in Israel are Arab families, and Arab municipalities constitute the poorest municipalities within Israel.[101]"

Since there is no Israeli population that Palestinians have colonized and made into a minority that is subject to systemic discrimination, the mistreatment of Palestinian citizens of Israel provides another example where the narrative of Israelis and Palestinians reciprocally harming one another does not stand up to scrutiny.

RESPONSIBILITY

Of the five editorials that the *Times* published during and immediately before Protective Edge, only the July 19th editorial
criticizes Israel, the United States, and the EU for undermining the
Palestinian and in this way helping precipitate the violence.[102]
During the war, for example, Hamas and its allies in Gaza considered non-interference in a Palestinian unity government a
condition for a ceasefire.[103] Keeping the unity government in the
background mitigates the degree to which readers are likely to
see the Palestinian grievances during Protective Edge as legitimate. To mention this crucial context for the fighting in 20% of the
editorials on Protective Edge is to suggest that the undermining
of the Palestinian national unity government is only of minimal
significance. Moreover, the capacity of Israel and its Western allies to shape who governs Palestinians demonstrates the weakness of the "both sides" narrative: only one side of Palestine-Israel has the capacity to obstruct the other's national unity and
manage their political affairs.

Furthermore, some examples of the "both sides" narrative
are premised upon the idea that the longer history of Palestine-Israel is one of mutual and roughly equal responsibility for
the absence of a just resolution. For instance, Gershon Baskin writes in *Slate* that Protective Edge was inevitable because

Israelis and Palestinians failed to "[move] forward on peace-making in the past, either through the efforts of U.S. Secretary of State John Kerry or through one of the numerous other missed opportunities."[104] Baskin goes on to argue that "we need a brave initiative and a courageous Arab leader (and Israeli one) to get beyond the current lose-lose scenario in progress." Similarly, a *Financial Times* editorial critical of Israeli conduct during Protective Edge says, "Of course, it would be naive to think there is an immediate political settlement available to the Israelis—if only they would grab it. In reality, a 'final status' agreement to the Israeli-Palestinian conflict remains very elusive—and the fault lies on both sides."[105]

It is inaccurate to say that, over the longer-term, both sides are equally responsible for the absence of peace and justice. The first major, direct negotiations between Israel and the Palestinians took place in Madrid in 1991. The US agreed to Israeli Prime Minister Yitzhak Shamir's insistence that the Palestine Liberation Organization (PLO) be excluded from the talks, even though the PLO was the principle representative of the Palestinians, and that the Palestinian delegation be subject to Israeli approval. Furthermore, the US and Israel decided that the formal agenda would not include Palestinian desires for independence and statehood.[106] Little was accomplished by these talks. In the early 1990s, the PLO did have secret, direct negotiations with

Israel in Washington and in Oslo. These discussions led to the Oslo Accords, which in September of 1993 were famously sealed on the White House lawn by a handshake between PLO Chairman Yasser Arafat and Israeli Prime Minister Yitzhak Rabin. The Oslo Declaration of Principles (DOP) acknowledged that the Palestinians are a distinct people, recognized the PLO as their representatives, and agreed that Gaza and the West Bank are a single territorial unit, establishing a Palestinian authority to partially govern these lands. The DOP does not grant the Palestinians territorial jurisdiction over the West Bank, Gaza, and East Jerusalem or accept that international occupation law applies to these places. Moreover, the DOP fails to note that Palestinians have the right to self-determination. It also delays discussion of key issues such as Israeli settlements and military installations until "final status" negotiations.[107] Nor does the DOP address the matter of Palestinian refugees. In the first twenty years after the accords were signed, the number of Israeli settlers more than doubled from 262,500 settlers in 1993 to over 520,000 in 2013 in the West Bank, including 200,000 in East Jerusalem.[108] The Oslo agreements, Linda Tabar writes, "proved to be a recipe for perpetual Israeli settler colonial domination over Palestinian lives," explaining that "The overlapping apparatuses which were introduced in the name of 'peace-building,' disciplined colonised Palestinians within a deepening system of

43

Zionist settler colonial rule and capitalist penetration."[109] In the Camp David negotiations in the year 2000, which were supposedly an attempt to reach a final status agreement, US President Bill Clinton and Israeli Prime Minister Ehud Barak asked Arafat to forsake the right of the refugees Israel expelled in 1948 to return and again offered limited sovereignty in the West Bank and Gaza and Arafat refused.[110]

During George W Bush's presidency, the offers made to Palestinians were no better. In a 2004 letter to Israeli Prime Minister Ariel Sharon, Bush avoided describing Israeli settlements as illegal and called them "realities" that would have to be taken into account.[111] In American-mediated Palestinian-Israeli talks, US Secretary of State Condoleezza Rice pressed the Palestinians to drop the refugee issue and to accept the presence of Israeli troops and asked Palestinians to allow Israel to keep large chunks of land in West Bank settlements such as Ariel and Maale Adumim, which would split a hypothetical Palestinian state into at least four easily isolated cantons.[112]

When Barak Obama became president, his government did not embark on a substantially different course in its policies toward Palestinian-Israeli negotiations. Obama appointed George Mitchell as the presidential special envoy to deal with the issue. Even though Hamas represents many Palestinians, Mitchell forbade the group from participating in talks unless it

met conditions such as the renunciation of violence, a require-
ment which was not applied to Israel.[113] Dennis Ross took over
Obama's Palestine-Israel file from Mitchell. Ross asked Israel to
freeze settlement building for a mere three months in exchange
for twenty F-35 stealth attack jets and a US veto of the planned
Palestinian statehood bid at the UN. Israel refused even that.[114]
The Obama administration opposed the Palestinian bid anyway.
In 2013-14 talks that US Secretary of State John Kerry supervised, a key US mediator in charge of the discussions was Martin
Indyk, a longtime pro-Israel lobbyist.[115] During these talks, Netanyahu demanded that Palestinians give up on the right of the
refugees to return to their homes[116] and Israel announced that it
would build 1,400 new settlement homes on the very land whose
future was supposedly being negotiated.[117] The Israeli government also said that it would not agree to the Palestinians having
a state on the 1967 borders and insisted on its right to keep its
massive separation wall.[118]

In each of the major negotiations, there is scant evidence that
Israeli leaders were genuinely committed to ending their denial
of Palestinian rights, a necessary precondition for a resolution to
the Palestine-Israel question. Thus it is more accurate to say that
it is because of the Israeli state and its American backers' commitment to maintaining Israeli control over Palestine that there
is no peace. It is not accurate to say, as the *Financial Times* does,

that "the fault lies on both sides" or to suggest as Baskin does that the status of Palestine remains in doubt because Israelis and Palestinians have both missed opportunities and lacked courageous leaders.

A MORE ACCURATE POINT OF DEPARTURE:

Commentary should at a minimum refrain from distorting what has happened between Israelis and Palestinians by describing it as a conflict for which "both sides" bare comparable responsibility and in which both sides have suffered to comparable extents. As I have shown, the evidence does not support such a perspective. The scholarly research, reports from human rights groups, and findings of international institutions that I have discussed make it clear that the Israeli state has colonized and oppressed Palestinians.

Instead of the "both sides" narrative, a more accurate point of departure would be, as Taraki suggests, "that the main features of the situation in Palestine/Israel today are defined by and have their roots in the dispossession of two-thirds of the indigenous population; the institutionalized denial to non-Jews of the full rights of citizenship in a Jewish state; and the relentless drive to ensure a Jewish majority in historic Palestine."[119] Primary fault for violence in a colonial situation by definition lies with the colonizer and the colonized population by definition suffers more than that of colonizers, making the "both sides" narrative untenable on its face.

It is true that there are Israeli civilians who have been killed and maimed by Palestinians, albeit with less frequency and in far smaller numbers than Israelis have done to Palestinians, but this does not make the "both sides" narrative that I have been criticizing an accurate way of telling the story. If all that is necessary for a "both sides" frame to be considered illuminating is for *any* amount of pain to be experienced by people in both groups and *any* amount of misdeeds to be carried out by all the relevant actors, irrespective of the proportion or context, then virtually all political violence in human history can be reduced to tales in which all of the involved groups both suffer and share blame for the fighting regardless of questions of scale, cause and effect, and power differentials. Analysis is socially useful when it enables readers to grasp the particulars of contentious issues, to understand the power relations that produce these matters, and to question what can be done to change them. The "both sides" narrative does the opposite.

Ibrahim Abu-Lughod writes that while there are two distinct peoples on the land of Palestine in search of political sovereignty, "The historic politics of negation would deny one of these two peoples their aspiration."[120] The "both sides" narrative is one form that the politics of negation takes. This paradigm rests on erasing wrongs that have been done to Palestinians as well as erasing rights to which they are entitled according to any coherent sense of justice, such as the right of refugees to return, the right to self-determination, the right not to be occupied by a military, and the right not to be second class citizens.

Presenting Palestine-Israel as a story of two sides who have committed wrongs and been wronged to similar degrees is de-mobilizing. This narrative suggests that both groups have equally serious grievances and are equally culpable for ongoing violence, which points to the erroneous conclusion that Palestine-Israel can be solved by insisting that both parties need to make a comparable number of concessions. In this way, propagating the idea that Palestine-Israel ought to be viewed through the "both sides" frame, rather than as a story of Israel colonizing Palestinians, inhibits popular willingness to take actions that can contribute to a just peace.

CHAPTER TWO: EXTREMISTS AND MODERATES

In a June 7, 2014 editorial critical of the Fatah-Hamas unity deal, whose demise preceded that summer's war, *The New York Times'* editorial board sympathizes with Israeli Prime Minister Benjamin Netanyahu's declaration that Israel will not negotiate with a Palestinian government that includes Hamas. Though the *Times* notes that Netanyahu's government had previously negotiated with Hamas, the editors write that "Mr. Netanyahu is correct that Hamas, the Iran-backed group that took control of the Gaza Strip in 2007, is a violent, extremist organization."[1] The editorial then says that "While Hamas cannot simply be wished away, the United States and other countries that consider Hamas a terrorist group may find it impossible to continue aiding the Palestinians if Hamas plays a more pronounced role." The editors, furthermore, lament "Hamas's hatred of Israel." The *Times* goes on to say that, if the US is to support the Palestinian unity government, it "has to be careful to somehow distinguish between its support for the new government and an endorsement of Hamas and its violent, hateful behaviour." Hamas is consistently described as violent, hateful, and terroristic but Israel is not described this way, even though the latter has ethnically-cleansed, colonized, occupied, and erected a system of institutional discrimination against the Palestinians. In this regard, the discourse about "extremists and moderates" in Palestine-Israel is a continuation of that of other colonial and imperial situations: when the oppressed use force it is "hateful" violence and when the oppressor uses vastly more destructive force it is not. This framing conceals that Palestinians, like any occupied or colonized people, have the right to armed resistance under international law. For example, in 1974 the UN General Assembly affirmed "the legitimacy of the peoples' struggle for liberation form [sic] colonial and foreign domination and alien subjugation by all available means, including armed struggle."[2] The General Assembly has re-affirmed that right on numerous occasions.

In the *Times'* 7 August 2014 editorial, the editors write that "In too many cases, Israel launched weapons that hit schools and shelters and failed to adequately protect Palestinian citizens. But Hamas knowingly targeted Israeli civilian centers in violation of any civilized standard."[3] In the first part of this excerpt, readers are told that Israeli attacks "hit schools and shelters" but the editors offer no comment on whether Israel struck such targets intentionally and they use no modifiers that indicate a judgment about the harm these actions caused or about the nature of those who took them. When Israel is criticized it is for "fail[ing[to adequately protect Palestinian citizens." Setting aside that Palestinians in Gaza are not "citizens" of any state and that this is a major reason that there is violence in the first place, this excerpt is notable for the way that it presumes Israel is attempting to protect Palestinians even though there is ample evidence that suggests otherwise. When such language is used to mildly criticize Israel, it functions to shore up the image of Israel as well-intentioned, civilized, and moderate. Yet Hamas' rocket fire, though it injured or killed very few people, is described as intentional and denounced in the strongest possible terms: it is "a violation of any civilized standard." The rebukes given to Israel and Hamas are completely out of proportion with the level of harm attributable to either party. Such rhetoric suggests that the colonized Palestinians and their backers are uncivilized savages and, since no comparable terminology is applied to Israel, the Israeli colonizers and their patrons are enlightened and civilized.

The *Times'* editors, furthermore, write that "Israel is not going away. But neither are the Palestinians, and the extremists among them will always find a place and an audience if there is no hope and no responsible moderate leaders to point the way." This formulation de-humanizes the Palestinians: they need "hope," according to the *Times*, not because they are as deserving as political rights as any other group but because absent that hope they could become dangerous extremists. Even as the paper advocates better conditions for the Palestinians, the subtext is that such changes are necessary because hopeless Palestinians are a threat to Israel. In these respects, this passage contributes to the notion that Palestine-Israel is a story about "extremists and moderates." At the same time that Palestinians are de-humanized, they are also infantalized: without the tutelage of "responsible" leaders, they are at risk of irresponsible extremism. The language that categorizes Arabs as either "responsible" or irresponsible is the language of colonialism and imperialism. No definition of "responsible" is offered but it is clear that this American newspaper claims for itself the authority to set the terms under which Palestinians must conduct themselves. Moreover, the same article declares that "Rocket attacks into Israel by Hamas and other extremist groups must stop, along with other terrorist attacks." At no point in the editorial is Israeli violence described as "terrorist" and neither is the Israeli state considered extremist even though it has killed and injured far more people than any of the Palestinian armed factions. In this way, the story being told about Protective Edge is that it as a war between Palestinian extremists and an Israeli state that is apparently moderate.

The *Times*' 19 July 2014 editorial describes Hamas' actions as "terror" three times, in one case in the form of an approving quote of Obama, and does not describe Israel's violence in the same terms even though the latter kills and injures far more civilians. The paper says that "another ceasefire might be the best that anyone can hope for at this moment. But Hamas leaders have rejected one proposed in the past week by Egypt and are demanding better terms. Meanwhile, Palestinian civilians suffer the consequences." The paper criticizes Hamas for rejecting the ceasefire but does not mention its substance. Israel and Egypt, two of Hamas' main enemies, drew up the ceasefire without Hamas being involved.[4] The proposal offered no concrete steps for lifting the US-Israeli-Egyptian siege of Gaza[5] and Netanyahu suggested that the agreement would be used to completely disarm Gaza.[6] Given that Israeli and Egyptian militaries and security apparatuses enforce the siege through violence, it is inaccurate to describe a proposal that leaves in place the siege as a "ceasefire." By excluding these details and making an unqualified reference to a "ceasefire," it sounds as if it was unreasonable if not outright depraved for Gaza's militants to reject the offer. Thus the *Times* represents Israel as a rational actor that would prefer peace and Hamas as irrationally bent on violence. In the last two sentences of the passage the *Times* also implies that, because Hamas rejected the ceasefire offer, they are culpable for Palestinian civilian casualties.

Furthermore, the *Times* says in its 25 July 2014 editorial that "Hamas deserves scrutiny, as well as the strongest possible condemnation for storing and launching rockets in heavily populated areas, knowing full well they would draw Israeli fire to places where civilians live. Unlike Israel, Hamas has not built bomb shelters where civilians can seek refuge. And even as war rages and his people are exposed, Hamas's political leader, Khaled Meshal, has been safely ensconced at his exile home in Qatar."[7]

The notion that Hamas is liable for the killing of Palestinians and destruction of Gaza absolves Israel of responsibility for Palestinian suffering even as Israel bombed and besieged the Strip. Under international law, occupying powers such as Israel are responsible for the well-being of the population they occupy. While the *Times* asserts that Hamas deserves "the strongest possible condemnation" for operating from populated areas, the harshest criticism of Israel in this article is when the editors say that "it is fair to ask whether Israel is doing enough to prevent" Palestinian civilians from being harmed. That the language used to fault Israel for Palestinian hardship is much softer than that which is used to fault Hamas indicates that the *Times* believes Hamas is the main reason that Palestinians are suffering. The paper's August 7, 2014 editorial, furthermore, says that Hamas "launched weapons from populated areas in what looks like a deliberate effort to draw Israeli fire on innocents." In this framing, Israel is forgiven for killing Palestinian civilians while Hamas is held responsible. By suggesting that Hamas is to blame for the deaths of their own people, the paper contributes to the narrative that Hamas is an atavistic group committed to violence for its own sake who must therefore be dealt with violently.

15 MILLION JEWS AND A HUNDRED TIMES AS MANY MUSLIMS

It is more often the Palestinians who are reduced to religious zealots than the Israelis. In such cases, the "extremists and moderates" narrative favors Israel by presenting it as contending with theocratic fundamentalists who cannot be reasoned with let alone be expected to abide by a resolution under which Arabs and Jews might live together peacefully and as equals.

The religious extremists narrative, I will show, errs by abstracting religious devotion from the social factors with which it interplays. Such perspectives point audiences toward overly simplistic perspectives while obscuring a wealth of important aspects of Palestine-Israel that need to be comprehended in order to understand the issue.

In November 2014, two Palestinians killed five Israelis, including four rabbis, in a Jerusalem synagogue. Following the attack, Anshel Pfeffer,[8] a correspondent for *Ha'aretz*, wrote in *The Guardian* that "This is what a religious war looks like, and we should stop kidding ourselves that this is not what has been happening in the Middle East." Pfeffer describes the notion that Palestine-Israel is a fight over territory as a "charade" and "the sheikhs and rabbis" as "the real movers in the wars of hate." He then writes that "Accepting that the Palestine-Israel conflict is also a bitter religious war runs counter to the international community's preferred solutions . . . which is a central reason that none of these solutions have worked." He also claims that whereas "most Israelis abhor" acts such as the burning of Palestinian mosques "even a cursory glance at the Palestinian media reveals a glorification of attacks against Jews."

Sam Harris, the neuroscientist and bestselling atheist pundit, was on a podcast during Protective Edge that was then turned into a widely circulated blog post entitled "Why Don't I Criticize Israel?"[9] Harris frames his discussion of Palestine-Israel around religion from the outset when he says that he has criticized "both Israel and Judaism" but has "kept some sense of proportion. There are something like 15 million Jews on earth at this moment; there are a hundred times as many Muslims." He then explains why he thinks Judaism is less bad than Islam or Christianity. In his view, the question of Palestine is not only a religious conflict between Israelis and Palestinians but a conflict between

Muslims and Jewish people in general. The facts that there are approximately half a million Palestinian Christians and that most Jewish people do not live in Israel go unmentioned. Harris further claims that "incompatible religious attachments to this land have made it impossible for Muslims and Jews to negotiate like rational human beings, and they have made it impossible for them to live in peace."

In Ali A. Rizvi's *Huffington Post* article, which was also written during Protective Edge, the author asserts that "Palestinian supporters would be just as ardently pro-Israel if they were born in Israeli or Jewish families, and vice versa."[10] He claims that "most people's view of this conflict are largely accidents of birth" and he writes twice that it is "at its core, a tribal conflict." His article has a subheading entitled "Why does everyone keep saying this is not a religious conflict?" This section begins with quotes from the Old Testament about God promising Israel to the Jewish people followed by excerpts from the Quran. He quotes one excerpt telling Muslims not to ally with Jews or Christians and another that is explicitly anti-Semitic, which tells Muslims to kill Jews and was quoted in the charter Hamas had when Rizvi wrote the article. Rizvi then asks: "Please tell me—in light of these passages written centuries and millennia before the creation of Israel or the occupation—how can anyone conclude that religion isn't at the root of this, or at least a key driving factor?"

A *Washington Post* editorial written during Protective Edge questions a proposal put forth by US Secretary of State John Kerry, which Turkey and Qatar supported, under which government employees in Gaza would be paid and Gaza's border would be opened. The *Post*'s criticism is that this proposal "had the effect of sidelining the secular governments of Egypt and Mr. Abbas, which stand on the other side of the Middle East's divide between pro and anti-Islamist forces."[11] Thus the paper argues that the diverse array of political forces across the entire region, including Palestine, can be neatly categorized as either Islamist or secular and that religiosity is the operative issue in all of the nations in the Middle East.

The fall of 2015 saw intensified Palestinian unrest wherein Israeli police and soldiers killed many Palestinians and Israelis were killed by Palestinians, typically with knives in "lone wolf" attacks apparently not orchestrated by any Palestinian political organization. In an *Atlantic* article published at the time, Jeffrey Goldberg blames Mahmood Abbas, head of the Palestinian Authority, for inciting the bloodshed by spreading false rumors that Israel wanted to interfere with Muslim worship and contends that the Israeli settlement movement:

> obscures what might be the actual root cause of the
> Middle East conflict: the unwillingness of many Muslim

> Palestinians to accept the notion that Jews are a people
> who are indigenous to the land Palestinians believe to be
> exclusively their own, and that the third-holiest site in
> Islam is also the holiest site of another religion, one whose
> adherents reject the notion of Muslim supersessionism.[12]

He ends his article by essentially repeating the same claim: "The violence of the past two weeks . . . is rooted not in Israeli settlement policy, but in a worldview that dismisses the national and religious rights of Jews." In Goldberg's view, the 2015 violence cannot be traced to Israeli colonialism but to anti-Semitism and religious beliefs.

Similarly, in an article about Omar Mateen's mass murder of 49 people in the Florida LGBT nightclub Pulse, Nick Cohen argues that "In, Israel, Islamists murder Jews, because they are Jews"[13] as though killings of Israelis by Palestinians can be solely attributed to the religious beliefs of Israelis.

I am not suggesting that none of these articles acknowledge that non-religious factors shape Palestine-Israel. My point is that they all suggest that religion is a central cause, if not the central cause, and say very little about issues such as colonization and geopolitics.

In several instances, casting Palestine-Israel as a religious conflict this leads commentators to conclude that Israel is more worthy of support than the Palestinians.

In an article published in the midst of Protective Edge, James Bloodworth writes that "Building settlements on stolen land is an affront to Palestinian self-determination, but then the virulent anti-Semitism of Hamas is also a threat to Israel." He invokes the slogan "fascism means war" and asks, "What ever happened to that? This is as true today as it ever was. Get over the idea that fascism is restricted to white men flinging their arms in the air and shouting 'sieg heil.' Fascists can have brown faces too."[14] This passage suggests that Hamas is an anti-Semitic fascist group and that Israel's attack on Gaza therefore deserves support.

Rizvi also implies that anti-Semitism is the key factor behind criticisms of Israel that come from Muslims. He writes that Muslims' outrage at Israeli conduct during Protective Edge was more intense than was Muslims' condemnation of the killings that the Syrian government and the Islamic State group were carrying out at the same time. He writes that this apparent discrepancy "clearly points to the likelihood that the Muslim world's opposition to Israel isn't just about the number of dead" and that "If I were Assad or ISIS right now, I'd be thanking God I'm not Jewish." Furthermore, Rizvi asks people from countries with Muslim majorities: "if Israel withdrew from the occupied territories tomorrow . . . *and* went back to the 1967 borders—*and* gave the Palestinians East Jerusalem—do you honestly think Hamas wouldn't find something else to pick a fight about? Do you honestly think that this has absolutely nothing to do with the fact that they are Jews?" These rhetorical questions clearly imply that, in his view, Hamas opposes Israel not only because of the occupation but also because of a hatred of Jewish people. He goes on to write that "Yes, there's an unfair and illegal occupation there, and yes, it's a human rights disaster. But it is also true that much of the other side is deeply driven by anti-Semitism." These comments are in a section of his article called "Why is everything so much worse when there are Jews involved?" Like Harris, Rizvi presents the struggle for historic Palestine as one between Jews and Muslims writ large rather than one between Israelis and Palestinians.

Harris' thesis in "Why Don't I Criticize Israel" is that Israel deserves support because, in his estimation, religious fanaticism is more common among Palestinians than Israelis and because he believes that the religious fanaticism of Palestinians and Muslims in other countries is the main reason there is no peace in Palestine-Israel. He claims that "you have to side with Israel here" because "You have one side [Israel] which if it really could accomplish its aims would simply live peacefully with its neighbors, and you have another side [Palestinians] which is seeking to implement a seventh century theocracy in the Holy Land." Moreover, he asserts that "Palestinian terrorism (and Muslim anti-Semitism) is what has made peaceful coexistence thus far impossible" and that, while illegal Israeli settlements should be opposed, "Absent Palestinian terrorism and Muslim anti-Semitism, we could be talking about a 'one-state solution,' and the settlements would be moot." Harris' blog, furthermore, casts Palestine-Israel as a sub-set of a clash of civilizations between the rational, secular West and fundamental-ist Muslims. He says that Israel is morally superior to its antago-nists since Hamas and "Muslims in other recent conflicts, in Iraq and elsewhere" use people from their own communities as human shields even though, two days before Harris' blog was published, Amnesty International said it "does not have evidence at this point that Palestinian civilians have been intentionally used by Hamas or Palestinian armed groups during the current hostilities to 'shield' specific locations or military personnel or equipment from Israeli attacks.[15] "The Muslims," he writes, "are acting on the assumption—the knowledge, in fact—that the infidels with whom they fight, the very people whom their religion does nothing but vilify, will be deterred by their use of Muslim human shields. They consider the Jews the spawn of apes and pigs—and yet they rely on the fact that they don't want to kill Muslim noncombatants" although the UN[16] would later find that Israeli forces used Pales-tinian civilians as human shields. He goes on to explain that "The term 'Muslims' in this paragraph means 'Muslim combatants' of the sort that Western forces have encountered in Iraq, Afghani-stan, and elsewhere." He claims, furthermore, that "Even on their worst day, the Israelis act with greater care and compassion and self-criticism than Muslim combatants have anywhere, ever." In the penultimate paragraph, he asks, "What do groups like ISIS and al-Qaeda and even Hamas want? They want to impose their religious views on the rest of humanity. They want to stifle every freedom that decent, educated, secular people care about." For Harris:

> This is the great story of our time. For the rest of our lives, and the lives of our children, we are going to be confronted by people who don't want to live peacefully in a secular, pluralistic world, because they are desperate to get to Paradise, and they are willing to destroy the very possibility of human happiness along the way. The truth is, we are all living in Israel.

HAMAS IN CONTEXT

Such simplistic, de-contextualized commentary on Hamas does not help readers comprehend the group. As Joel Beinin argues, "The discourse of terrorism precludes analysis linking Palestinian violence to Israeli actions."[17] The limits of framing Hamas as merely a terrorist organization are readily apparent in that it has not carried out any attack outside of historic Palestine and Syria. After 9/11, notably, a Hamas leaflet denounced the attacks as "violence against innocent civilians."[18] Hamas are central actors in contemporary Palestine-Israel and the public who are consuming news media about the issue need a more thorough understanding of the group and the contexts in which it exists. It is true that Hamas' charter contained anti-Semitic language, which has now been removed.[19] Many Israeli groups and politicians have also made racist utterances. In neither case are these statements by themselves a sufficient basis for analysis of the relevant actors.

Hamas was initially a branch of the Muslim Brotherhood and began to gain strength during the First Intifada, which started in 1987. Hamas' objectives were in tension with those of the secular nationalist movement that dominated Palestinian politics at the time, the PLO. Whereas the PLO wanted to negotiate a two state solution with Israel that was based on the 1967 borders, Hamas sought to rid all of historic Palestine of Zionism and "incorporated the imperative of liberating Muslim holy land into national goals."[20] The history of Hamas is inseparable from that of the Oslo process. At first, the 1993 Oslo Accords were reasonably popular among Palestinians and Hamas' opposition to the agreements marginalized Hamas. In 1996 Mahmud Zahbar, a Hamas leader in Gaza, advocated building social infrastructure linked to the group's political-religious goals by establishing Islamic charities, orphanages, and community events. By 1999, Hamas' charities ran 65 percent of Gaza's primary schools.[21] Though Hamas resolutely opposed the PA and though the PA repeatedly unleashed its security forces against Hamas, which led to violence, the latter opposed a Palestinian civil war on religious and political grounds.[22]

Hamas' violence can only be understood in the context of Israeli violence. As Khaled Hroub argues, "the radicalism of Hamas should be seen as a completely predictable result of the ongoing Israeli colonial project. Palestinians support whichever movement holds the banner of resistance against that occupation and promises to defend the Palestinian rights of freedom and self-determination."[23] The group's first suicide attacks were "launched in retaliation for the Hebron massacre" in which the American-Israeli Baruch Goldstein killed 29 Palestinians and wounded 125 others who had gathered to pray inside the Ibrahimi Mosque at the Cave of the Patriarchs compound.[24] In August 1995, Hamas abided by a tacit ceasefire with Israel in advance of the Taba accords, which were to occur under the auspices of Oslo, until Israel killed Hamas military leader Yahya 'Ayyash on January 6th 1996 and Hamas retaliated by bombing Israeli buses in February and March of that year.[25] In that period, Israel arrested thousands of Hamas activists.[26] Beinin explains that the violence of that timeframe "was largely due to failure to resolve the political issues left open by the Israeli-PLO agreements, the expansion of settlements, and the deteriorating economic conditions of Palestinians."[27]

When Ariel Sharon visited the al-Aqsa mosque in September 2000 and ignited the Second Intifada, the Israeli military snipers' rules of engagement stipulated that any Palestinians over the age of 12 were fair targets.[28] Meanwhile Israel increased the rate at which they demolished Palestinians houses and assassinated Palestinian political activists in a period that Charmaine Seitz characterizes as one of "unprecedented bloodshed, almost entirely on the Palestinian side."[29] Hamas did not join the fighting until January 2001 when its 'Izz al-Din al-Qassam Brigades claimed responsibility for the shooting two Israelis in the West Bank city Tulkarm.[30] On February 14th, Hamas said it was one of its members who drove a bus into a crowd of Israelis in occupied Gaza and killed 8, some of whom were soldiers while others were not.[31] A suicide bombing in Jerusalem in March killed three Israelis and another suicide bombing, this one in a Tel Aviv nightclub, killed 21 and Hamas claimed responsibility.[32] Hamas justified these actions by saying that, as long as Israel was killing Palestinian civilians, Israeli civilians would be treated the same way.[33] Seitz assesses matters in the following terms: "As Israel bombarded and encircled Palestinian institutions and security installations, the only countervailing [Palestinian] force was armed activity."[34] In just under a year and a half, Israel ordered 175 assassinations against Palestinians activists of various political stripes, injuring 310 and killing 235 and 79 of the dead were not even the intended targets: the assassinations created a desire for revenge among Palestinians and drew more of them into armed struggle; several of those who carried out attacks on Israelis had just had a friend or relative killed by Israel.[35] After the 9/11 attacks, the US brokered a meeting between Arafat and Israeli Foreign Minister Shimon Peres who agreed that the Palestinians would restore security coordination with Israel while Israel would lift its closure that blocked trade between Palestinian towns. Israel failed to lift the closure and killed 20 Palestinians in raids. After that, Hamas's Qassam Brigades sent two Palestinians to kill two young Israelis in an illegal settlement in occupied Gaza.[36] Media outlets disorient their readers when they remove Israeli actions from the equation and present Hamas violence as though it takes place in a vacuum. Situating Hamas' conduct in relation to Israel's would provide media audiences with the multi-dimensional perspective necessary to make sense of what happens in Palestine-Israel.

It is a mistake to portray Hamas as a group that is singularly driven by religious dogma. It has shown itself to be a pragmatic political organization as well. During the 2006 campaign, it supported Christian candidates and, when the group won the election, it appointed a Christian to its cabinet as the Minister of Tourism.[37] Similarly, Hamas' social work, which has helped the poor and supported thousands of Palestinians, has won it considerable popularity.[38] It is true that there was a religious dimension to the Second Intifada, the period that preceded Hamas' 2006 election victory. Re-runs of the al-Aqsa clash took place at other places with religious significance. There was fighting at a site in Nablus that some orthodox Jews regard as the site of Joseph's tomb while Jewish people burned mosques in Palestinian-Israeli towns and Palestinians burned the Jericho synagogue. Moreover, according to Seitz, the PA leadership deployed religious symbols and rhetoric in what was likely "an admission of weakness against the strengthened narrative of irredentist religious struggle."[39]

Yet it is a mistake to suggest that religiosity arises outside of any material circumstance. In the 1980s, Israel helped to encourage religious groups in Gaza in order to create a counterweight to the secular nationalists of the Palestine Liberation Organization, which was then the dominant faction in Palestinian politics.[40] During the Second Intifada, Seitz points out, an important reason that Hamas gained strength was that Israel's strategy was to dismantle the quasi-national Palestinian institutions created during Oslo and Hamas was able to fill the void with its networks.[41] Seitz writes that, during the Second Intifada, Palestinian society increasingly turned to religion as a way to create meaning for its immense losses and to navigate its difficult daily life, which is evident in an almost 50 percent increase in mosque attendance in the first four years of the uprising.[42] Pappe describes religion as "an effective response to the pressures of endless uprooting, deprivation and discrimination" that Palestinians have experienced.[43] He argues that religion also "offered a redemptive outlook on life for Jews in Israel, who were living under less harsh conditions [than Palestinians] but were nonetheless experiencing dismay and frustration born out of economic hardship."[44] In Palestinian rural areas, traditional beliefs that had been strong for centuries were easily channeled into politics, given Israeli encroachment into the lives of this portion of the Palestinian population.[45] A parallel tendency prevailed in poor urban neighbourhoods such as Nazareth, Hebron, and Nablus; Palestinian political Islam first appeared in Wadi Ara' where life was even harder than in the refugee camps, in the inner cities, and in the villages of the West Bank and Gaza.[46] Moreover, the failure of the PLO to protect Palestinians from Israeli violence made political Islam attractive by comparison.[47] Hroub points out that, when Hamas was elected in 2006, their success was not because the Palestinian masses underwent an "overnight popular conversion to Hamas' religious fervor…. Christians and secular people voted for Hamas side by side with Hamas members."[48] These earthly reasons for the religious dimensions of Palestine-Israel indicate that it is wrong-headed to blame religion for continued violence without considering the material factors that help precipitate piety.

Hamas has substantial support among Palestinians. As Hroub writes, "there cannot be a sustainable and final peace deal without a real Palestinian consensus, to which Hamas's contribution is central." When news media reduce Hamas "to a mere 'terrorist group' whose only function is and has been to aimlessly kill Israelis," they are failing to inform their audience that "On the ground in their own country, Hamas has been seen by many Palestinians as a deeply entrenched socio-political and popular force."[49] By echoing US-Israeli demands that the group be sidelined, if not destroyed, such outlets are suggesting that a meaningful portion of the Palestinian population be deprived of its political representation. If journalists believe that killing civilians disqualifies Hamas from participating in political life, then one has to ask why those journalists do not regard the Israeli state's much longer history of killing far more civilians as de-legitimizing it and barring it from a role in resolving the outstanding issues with the Palestinians.

ISRAELI EXTREMISTS

Labelling particular Israelis "extremists" misleads readers in a different way. The *Times'* July 8, 2014 editorial on the killings of 3 Israeli and 1 Palestinian youth, which were part of the run-up to Operation Protective Edge, describes the killings as instances of "some people . . . act[ing] on extremist views. According to news reports, the suspects arrested in [Palestinian teenager Mohammed Abu] Khdeir's murder may be fans of a soccer club known for its anti-Arab rhetoric."[50] Condemning Israeli "extremists" for killing Palestinians without criticizing the policies of the Israeli state and its backers, who combine to kill far larger numbers of Palestinians than private Israeli citizens and who create a context in which people like Khdeir's killers operate, presents violence against Palestinians as exceptional rather than a central characteristic of Israeli settler-colonialism. Calling Khdeir's murders "extremists" implies that they are deviating from standard Israeli practices that are "moderate" and therefore rational, reasonable, and good.

The corollary to media coverage suggesting that Palestinians' cultural attitudes and religious beliefs are key reasons for the absence of peace is commentary that focuses its criticism of Israel on religious Jews. In an article published on the eve of Protective Edge, for instance, Jonathan Freedland writes that the impending violence could be especially deadly due to "a Jewish settler movement more aggressively messianist and bellicose than before" rather than the colonial policies of the Israeli state or the regional aims of its American patrons.[51]

Rizvi takes a similar approach when he suggests that religion is the only motivation for Israeli settlement building: "Settlement expansion is simply incomprehensible," he writes. "No one really understands the point of it. Virtually every US administration— from Nixon to Bush to Obama—has unequivocally opposed it.

There is no justification for it except a Biblical one . . ., which makes it slightly more difficult to see Israel's motives as purely secular."

Furthermore, Israel's Jewish extremists are the one aspect of the country that Harris condemns unequivocally. His criticisms of Israeli war crimes are qualified by remarks about Palestinians. He says that he does not give Israel a "pass to commit war crimes" but notes that such actions should be considered in the context of "the character of their enemies" and "the realities of living under the continuous threat of terrorism and of fighting multiple wars in a confined space." He argues that "Whatever terrible things the Israelis have done," they have nevertheless used restraint in so doing, and he says that Hamas deserves blame for the large number of Palestinian non-combatants killed by Israel because Hamas has not adequately protected Gaza's civilian population. He does, however, unconditionally denounce the elements of Israeli society that are strongly religious and says that he believes there are few such people in Israel. He writes that Jewish religious extremists are "truly dangerous," criticizes "Jews who are animated by their own religious hysteria and their own prophesies," and argues that "it is how Israel deals with these people—their own religious lunatics—that will determine whether they can truly hold the moral high ground." That Jewish fundamentalists are the only segment of Israeli society that

Harris opposes unreservedly indicates that he regards them as the only problematic part of Israel.

Describing small groups of Israelis as "extremists" presents the problem of Israeli violence toward Palestinians in individualistic rather than systemic terms. This framing suggests that the policies of the Israeli state and its backers are sound and that the problem is those who stray from these policies rather than the entire apparatus of Israeli dispossession and violence.

WHAT DRIVES THE VIOLENCE?

The "extremists and moderates" narrative that I have been discussing, particularly that branch of it that overstates the role of religion, downplays or outright evades political and economic factors driving the violence between Israelis and Palestinians. Specifically, this commentary pays insufficient attention to the ways that American foreign policy and Israeli settler-colonial capitalism shape what happens across historic Palestine. In this section, I will demonstrate the ways that such forces, which are central to what happens in Palestine-Israel, have prevented a just peace and that therefore media figures tell the wrong narrative when they present Palestine-Israel as a story about "extremists and moderates."

One crucial factor driving the violence in historic Palestine is that Israel is dependent on the US, which orients its client toward militarization. During the Cold War, Israel served as a US proxy. While the US-Israeli "special relationship" consolidated in 1967, America has funded Israel for much longer. Even before the 1967 war, the US gave Israel more aid per capita than the US gave any other country.[52] In 1957, US President Dwight D Eisenhower articulated the Eisenhower Doctrine, a declaration of US support for any Middle Eastern government that it considered targeted by "overt armed aggression from any nation controlled by International Communism."[53] Eisenhower's Secretary of State John Foster Dulles considered states in the region allied with the USSR to be "controlled by International Communism" and this included Egypt, which was one of Israel's primary adversaries at the time.[54] America was arming Middle Eastern states at odds with Egypt such as Saudi Arabia, Iran, and Jordan and in the late 1950s the US clandestinely allowed its ally in West Germany to ship American-made M-48 tanks to Israel.[55] A 1958 US National Security Council document says that a "logical corollary" of opposing what they thought of as radical Arab nationalism "would be to support Israel as the only strong pro-West power left in the Near East."[56] In the early 1960s, the Kennedy administration sent Hawk anti-aircraft missiles to Israel and the Johnson government sent A-4 Skyhawk attack bombers.[57] By 1967,

US planners saw Israel as useful for preventing the disruption of oil supplies and as a CIA proxy for carrying out American operations in the Middle East such as arming US-allied Kurdish forces or assisting the security forces of Iran, which was a US client at the time.[58]

The 1967 war cemented the US-Israeli relationship as the US came to see Israel as an indispensable tool against the USSR's Egyptian and Syrian allies. The Americans even sent Israel weapons that the US would not give its NATO partners.[59] A similar example is the 1968-70 War of Attrition wherein Egyptian, Jordanian, and PLO forces attempted to force Israel out of the Sinai, which it occupied in 1967. In the War of Attrition, Israel shot down several of the Soviet pilots who were participating in the war on the Egyptian side and killed many Soviet advisors to Egyptian air defence crews while America delivered state-of-the-art military equipment to Israel.[60] When Soviet-allied Syria attempted to support the Palestinians who were being massacred by Jordan during 1970's Black September, Israel prevented Syria from doing so on the US's behalf. During the 1973 war, American maneuvering brought the world to the edge of nuclear war: when Israel refused to obey a UN-mandated ceasefire, the Soviets placed their paratroopers on alert and shipped nuclear weapons to their forces on the Mediterranean.[61] The Soviet leadership called for a joint US-Soviet intervention to end the war and said the USSR would intervene alone if the US refused.[62] When the US and USSR were about to undertake this cooperation, the US instead put its worldwide armed forces on a general nuclear alert and only called on Israel to end its attacks at the last moment.[63] In 1974, the PLO signalled its willingness to accept a two state solution but Israel opposed the idea and the US "underwrote Israel's intransigence."[64]

After the Shah of Iran, one of America's most useful proxies, was overthrown in 1979, Israel became even more important to the US.[65] Starting with the 1967 occupation and throughout the 1970s, Israeli military attacks and assassinations decimated left wing and Arab nationalist movements across the Middle East that were threats to US client states.[66] It was with full US support that Israel invaded Lebanon in 1982 and attacked the PLO, Lebanese leftists, and the Syrian army, all of whom were Soviet allies, to say nothing of thousands of Palestinian and Lebanese civilians.[67] The US itself bombed Lebanon from the sea and sent troops into the country as part of its effort to install a government in Lebanon that would be friendly to the US and Israel.[68] In these ways, American elites supported Israeli violence as a means of weakening the Soviet Union in the Middle East and beyond, and of weakening progressive and nationalist forces in the Middle East. These manifestations of the relationships between the US and Israeli ruling classes demonstrate that, as Bashir

Abu-Manneh writes, US imperialism should "come to be seen as an intrinsic factor in the shaping and development of both the Arab-Israeli conflict and the structure of the Israeli polity."[69] He goes on to point out that the US

> has been determining major economic and political outcomes in the Middle East since at least 1967, with Israel continuing to play a crucial role in their realization. In Israel-Palestine, this has meant that force and colonial peace have alternated as main instruments of policy, with the main objective being a constant: Jewish supremacy in Palestine—as much land as possible, as few Palestinians as possible. The United States has exploited this Zionist imperative for its own interests in the region, and has fostered a militarized and fundamentalist Israel in the process.[70]

There are pro-Israel lobby groups in Washington that urge American planners to adopt policies friendly to Israeli elites. However, as Chomsky argues, it is doubtful they would have much influence if Israel could not be used to support the US ruling class's "primary interest in the Middle East region, which is to maintain control over its energy reserves and the flow of petrodollars."[71]

The US has also militarized Israel because of services that Israel's ruling class has rendered beyond the Middle East.[72] Israel is one of the world's foremost purveyors of mercenaries who have shared their counterinsurgency knowledge with security forces in Taiwan,[73] Indonesia, the Philippines, and with narco militants and paramilitaries in Colombia.[74] Israel, furthermore, helped the US provide support to an assortment of African dictators including Haile Selassie in Ethiopia, Idi Amin in Uganda, Mobutu Sese Seko in the Congo (when it was still 'Zaire'), Jean-Bédel Bokassa of Central Republic, and the apartheid regimes in Zimbabwe (when it was still 'Rhodesia') and South Africa, despite bans against doing so in the latter two cases.[75] In Latin America, Israel acted as a US arms broker and proxy by selling weapons that, because of congressional legislation, the US often could not sell directly to the murderous military regimes in Argentina, El Salvador, Guatemala, Honduras, and Nicaragua.[76] Max Ajl points out that:

> In return for this mercenary work for the United States, a domestic elite in Israel grew richer, pulling in its cut from the military grants while also profiting from the perpetual state of warfare ensured by the colonial occupation and Israel's decision to treat those states across its northern armistice lines as enemies to be controlled

and destabilized rather than neighbors with whom to trade and live.[77]

That such militarism rewards the Israeli and American ruling classes incentivizes Israel to continue its violence against Palestinians and disincentivizes them against a peaceful settlement. What this history means is that Israeli violence against Palestinians could not occur at the level that it does without America providing it with the means to do so. It means that any story about the causes of bloodshed in Palestine-Israel that fails to highlight the US role in fueling the violence is incomplete.

While one major goal of US Cold War maneuvering was to keep the USSR from having significant influence in the Middle East,[78] the end of this period did not mean that the US changed course on Palestine-Israel because the US was in principle opposed to any radical nationalism, whether Soviet-influenced or not. In the post-Cold War era, Israel has remained as deeply integrated into the US-led empire as ever. Israel, for example, has observer status in NATO.[79] Elliot Systems Ltd, an Israeli firm involved in building the separation barrier in Palestine-Israel, has also contributed to the "security" of the US-Mexico border wall.[80] Laleh Khalili points out that Israel is also a "significant exporter of the counterinsurgency knowledge it has accumulated in Palestine."[81] In a world "where imperial control through military intervention continues apace," she writes, Palestine is "an archetypal laboratory and a crucial node of global counterinsurgencies."[82] For example, in 2002 the US "observed" the Israeli invasion of Jenin and "borrowed" its usage of bulldozers in the US-led war on Iraq.[83] Similarly, the US Law Enforcement Exchange Program teaches Israel's shoot-to-kill methods to American police and is supported by the Jewish Institute for National Security, which pays $5000 per person to train American law enforcement in Israel.[84] The Israeli ruling class enriches itself by sharing with other repressive forces the technology, personnel, and battlefield knowledge that it has tested in its Palestinian laboratory. Israel's security establishment has cited its supposed cultural knowledge of Arab fighting strategies as grounds to train US military forces for counterinsurgency in urban Iraq in a mock Arab town modeled on Ramallah in the Ze'elim military base in the Negev in return for US funding and building of parts of the base.[85]

US support for Israel should be seen in part as a way for the US to subsidize America's military industry. Between 1997 and 2007, Israel signed agreements for $10.50 billion worth of US weapons imports, more than any country other than Saudi Arabia.[86] In 2003, the American firm Lockheed Martin made 102 F-16s specifically designed for Israeli needs as part of a $4.5 billion deal between the company and the Israeli government: much of the money Israel paid to Lockheed in that transaction originated in the US as Foreign Military Financing (FMF).[87] The ways in which the US government enriches American military companies can only be understood when seen in the context of US policy across the Middle East. As Frida Berrigan writes, a major barrier to any shift in American policy toward Palestine-Israel is "financial pressures from a U.S military industrial complex accustomed to billions of dollars in sales to Israel and other Middle Eastern nations locked in a seemingly perpetual arms race with each other but all buying American and using FMF to pay the bills."[88] Abu-Manneh explains that:

> The dynamic of American Empire/Israeli colonialism is . . . circular: U.S support reinforces Israeli colonialism and occupation which bolsters Israeli militarization of state and society, which generates new ideological justifications and breeds new religious fanaticism, leading to further indigenous resistance and to more U.S interventions in the region.[89]

Israel is also the only country allowed by American law to build its domestic military industry using a large portion of the military aid it receives from the US. This right extends to developing Israeli weapons systems based on US designs and using American FMF money to purchase materials and conduct research and development for the purpose of developing its own military sector.[90] Thus, Israel has permission to manufacture and upgrade US military technology and, according to a 2007 Memorandum of Understanding, can spend 26.3 percent of the FMF it receives from America on weapons systems manufactured in Israel.[91] In these ways, US aid to Israel subsidizes both the American and Israeli ruling classes. Yet, Ajl points out, "the United States forbids Israel from manufacturing crucial heavy weaponry, such as fighter jets, in order to maintain control over Israel. . . . [I]t maintains a monopoly on many of the production lines the Israeli army needs, in order to maintain a veto over Israeli foreign policy."[92]

The fact that Israel is deeply integrated into western capitalism also helps explain the U.S-Israeli special relationship. Israel has, for instance, preferential trade agreements with both the EU and the US.[93] Accordingly, the American ruling class, and the global capitalist elite more generally, have material reasons to support Israel and to make the state profitable. The US-Israeli special relationship can also be explained in part by the links between the two countries' elites. As Nitzan and Bichler point out, "since the 1990s, Israel has emerged not only as a favourite destination for 'high-tech' investors, money managers, and illegal flight capital, but also as the source of much capital outflow, with locally based capitalists acquiring assets outside their country."[94] In 1995, Israel privatized Koor, a major holding company with a stake in the military industry, by selling it to the U.S.-based Disney family. Two years later, the Israeli government sold its 43 percent share in Bank Hapoalim (which in turn owned 20 percent of Koor) to a group headed by U.S. investor Ted Arison for over $1 billion.[95] In 2013, the American billionaire Warren Buffet spent $2 billion to take full control of the Israeli company Iscar Metalworking.[96] Three years later, he invested $5 million in Israel bonds, helped raise $60 million in one night for those bonds, and recommended that other investors put their money in Israel.[97] Facebook[98] has an office in Tel Aviv as does Google, which also has a location in Haifa.[99] HP has a lab in Israel that overlooks Haifa[100] and Apple's second largest research and development centre is in Herzliya, Israel.[101]

American support for Israel also needs to be seen as part of US capital's broader strategy for dominating the Middle East, which involves having as many pliable client states as possible. Israel is one of these and so are the undemocratic governments of countries such as Egypt, Jordan, and the countries that make up the Gulf Cooperation Council (GCC): Bahrain, Kuwait, Oman, Qatar, Saudi Arabia, and the United Arab Emirates

(UAE). Adam Hanieh describes US support for Israel since the late 1980s as:

> Pursu[ing] a policy of integrating its bases of support in the region within a single, neoliberal economic zone tied to the US through a series of bilateral trade agreements. This vision is aimed at promoting the free flow of capital and goods (but not necessarily labour) throughout the Middle East region. The region's markets will be dominated by US imports, while cheap labour, concentrated in economic "free" zones owned by regional and international capital, will manufacture low-cost exports destined for markets in the US, the EU, Israel, and the Gulf. A central component of this vision is the normalization and integration of Israel into the Middle East. The US envisions a Middle East resting upon Israeli capital in the West and Gulf capital in the East, underpinning a low-wage, neoliberal zone that spans the region. What this means is that Israel's historic destruction of Palestinian national rights must be accepted and blessed by all states in the region.

An example of this process is the Qualified Industrial Zones (QIZ) in Jordan and Egypt, which were created through economic agreements between the US, Israel, Jordan, and Egypt. Most of the QIZs contain textile factories that act as subcontractors for US firms like Walmart and GAP and the factories themselves are owned by international capital, mainly from the United Arab Emirates, Israel, China, Taiwan, and Korea.[102] Most of the workers are migrants from South Asia who are unprotected by labour laws, prevented from joining unions, make miniscule wages, get sexually assaulted and regularly beaten, work extremely long shifts, have their passports confiscated on arrival, and are forced to live in overcrowded and unclean conditions.[103] The agreements for building the QIZs contain the unusual clause that goods produced there can get duty-free status in the US if a certain proportion of the inputs are Israeli.[104] The QIZs, Hanieh writes, "are constructed to weld Israeli and Arab capital together, integrating them with the US market and the American empire, in the joint exploitation of cheap labour."[105] Similarly, the gigantic highways that run across the West Bank and that connect Israeli cities on the Mediterranean with settlements in the Jordan Valley are conduits for trade between Israel and the Gulf.[106] Normalization between Israel and the Gulf states under the auspices of the US Empire has also deepened in the context of each of these states' hostility to Hezbollah, Iran, and Syria.[107] A significant example is the Syrian war that began in 2011 wherein Iran and Hezbollah supported the Syrian government while Israel, the Gulf states, the US, Turkey, and Jordan supported the Syrian opposition.[108]

Shifting political and economic dynamics inside Israel also propel its policies toward killing and colonizing Palestinians. The 1967 Israeli occupation of the West Bank and Gaza Strip increased the size of Israel's "domestic" market and provided a cheap source of highly exploitable labour: by the mid-1980s Palestinians from the occupied territories made up 7 percent of the Israeli labour force and, by 1985, approximately one-third of the West Bank and Gaza labour force worked in Israel.[109] US-supported military production became central to Israel's political economy once the 1967 occupation began, as the state directed production to favored sections of Israeli industry, dynamics that became even more pronounced after the 1973 war, giving those layers of Israeli capital who were profiting from armaments a vested interest in maintaining control over the Occupied Territories and in remaining at war with the Palestinians and other countries in the region.[110] In this period, multiple strata of Israel's ruling class had an economic interest in maintaining the occupation.

A reorientation of the Israeli state took place, however, in the context of a serious financial crisis in Israel. From 1968-1985, Israeli military expenditures ran from 21.7-32.8 percent of GDP while in the rest of the developed capitalist world the range was 3-6 percent of GDP.[111] In 1983, the price of Israeli bank shares collapsed and that was followed by hyperinflation. The Israeli government adopted a neoliberal economic stabilization plan (ESP), involving reduced government subsidies, restrictions on wage growth, and privatization.[112] A shift took place in the mid to late 1980s as key sections of the Israeli elite came to view the occupation as a drag on profits because of the costs associated with the First Intifada. Occupation meant an Arab boycott, and many international firms saw investment in Israel as risky due to political instability.[113] By the 1990s, consequently, sections of the Israeli ruling class came to favor "peace" in the form of the Oslo process. From January 1995 to September 1996, foreign investors bought $2.9 billion in Israeli stocks. Foreign investment in the country went from $4.7 billion to $19.6 billion and prominent US corporations such as IBM, Intel, and Microsoft announced major investments in Israel.[114]

Supporting the "peace process" cannot be understood to mean that Israeli elites backed Palestinian freedom: the Oslo years represented a recalibrating of Israeli control over Palestinians rather than the end of control. Sectors of Israel's ruling class remained heavily invested in the military industry. Colonial violence was institutionalized to the point that, as of the mid-2000s, 150,000 Israeli households were economically dependent on the arms and security industry.[115] Accordingly, the Oslo process, as well as the years preceding and following it, saw portions of the Israeli elite favor Oslo as a "solution" to the Palestinian question that sought to mollify Palestinian and regional resistance to Israeli colonization while enabling Israel to manage and profit from Palestinian people, land, and resources. During the harsh repression of Palestinians in the 2000-2005 Second Intifada, Israeli elites enriched themselves spectacularly. The profits of the top twenty-five companies on the Tel Aviv Stock Exchange tripled between 2002-2003 while those of the country's major banks increased by 350 percent.[116] In 2003, the salaries of bank executives were a hundred times higher than the minimum wage, prompting Yoav Peled to observe that "With such an economic bonanza provided by the state, it is unsurprising that Israel's top capitalists have preferred not to rock the boat." Occupation and colonialism have not prevented the Israeli ruling class from enriching itself. In many ways, it has enriched itself precisely because of these conditions. Yet these incentives against changing the deadly status quo are obfuscated by narratives that blame extremists, rather than US-Israeli institutions, for the violence.

There are myriad other ways in which the Israeli ruling class has profited from colonization. Dispossessing Palestinians should be seen as an example of primitive accumulation, a process in which capital addresses its unending need for new markets to exploit by forcefully taking and commodifying resources, land being chief among them as land is the essential unit for capitalist development. As Joel Beinin writes, "no Israeli court has recognized the property rights of any of the hundreds of thousands of Palestinians who have resided in East Jerusalem and the West Bank since becoming refugees in 1948 and who owned land and buildings subsequently included in the territory of the state of Israel."[117] For instance, the Israeli government has expropriated almost 35 percent of East Jerusalem from Palestinians since Israel's 1967 annexation of the city in order to build new Jewish neighborhoods, including the construction of fifty-one thousand Jewish residencies, most of which have been state housing.[118] Whatever the Biblical echoes of the land in Jerusalem, the land is not taken over merely because of religious or tribal zeal. Land is also expropriated in historic Palestine because it is valuable.

The Jordan Valley offers another example of how Israeli takeovers of Palestinian land have been profitable for Israel. The valley was an important agricultural area for Palestinians in the West Bank until the occupation of the area in 1967 when the Israeli military evicted many of the farmers, took their land, built military-agricultural settlements, and then built agribusiness and civilian residences, while securing water, access routes, and other resources.[119] Now Palestinians in the occupied territories have to buy water from Israel. Since Israel occupied these territories in 1967, it has passed a series of military orders to bring the West Bank's water resources and infrastructure into the state's domain while the Oslo accords and their sequel, Oslo II, facilitate Israel's "illegal exercise of sovereign rights over the water resources in the OPT."[120] Similarly, in the West Bank and Gaza, utilities are supplied by Israeli companies, with the exception of a small amount of electricity that is generated in Gaza.[121]

Measures that Israel takes to abridge Palestinian freedom of movement are sometimes also real estate takeovers. The UN reports that when Israel expands its military checkpoints in the occupied territories, this usually entails the appropriation of Palestinian land located in the vicinity.[122] The massive wall that Israel has built in the West Bank is the most dramatic illustration of how Israeli barriers have the dual function of arbitrarily limiting Palestinians' right to free movement and appropriating Palestinian land for Israel, both of which are problems that the International Court of Justice notes in its 2004 Advisory Opinion. The court found the wall contrary to international law.[123]

Israel's ruling class profits in myriad ways from Palestinian un-freedom, but this crucial aspect of the story is hidden by narratives that present what has happened as being the result of "extremists." Short newspaper articles cannot be expected to provide anything approaching all of these details. News outlets can, however, note these crucial dynamics and at a minimum can refrain from attributing the lack of peace in Palestine-Israel to reductive narratives about moderates and extremists.

THE NEW YORK TIMES ON "MODERATE" PALESTINIANS

Another aspect of the "extremists and moderates" narrative is that it presents the Palestinian Authority (PA), or the Fatah faction that dominates it, as the "good," moderate Palestinians. Hamas, as well as other less powerful factions, are cast as the "bad," extremist Palestinians. This framing suggests that the key to peace in Palestine-Israel is negotiation between Israel and the PA to the exclusion of other Palestinian groups and that the PA deserves support from Israel's western backers so that it can exert hegemony within Palestinian politics. *The New York Times'* June 7, 2014 editorial on the Palestinian unity government ends by saying: "the United States and Europe must continue to insist" that Fatah leader Mahmoud Abbas stick to his promise that the unity government will continue Fatah's commitment to non-violence, recognition of Israel and cooperating in administering the West Bank through the PA and "not allow Hamas to get the upper hand."[124] Similarly, the *Times'* July 19, 2014 editorial on Protective Edge says that "The best solution" to Palestine-Israel "remains a peace agreement between Israel and the Palestinian Authority, headed by the Fatah faction, which operates in the West Bank."[125] The editors lament the demise of the Palestinian unity government on the grounds that it "could have been a chance to erode Hamas's political standing further and boost Palestinian moderates like Mr. Abbas."

Moreover, the *Times'* July 25, 2014 editorial says that "Perversely" Protective Edge seems to be strengthening Hamas while "Mahmoud Abbas, a moderate, is being faulted for not achieving a Palestinian state in negotiations with Israel. Israel's interest would be ill-served if Mr. Abbas ends up being marginalized while the hard-liners are empowered. Any cease-fire should be structured to help strengthen Mr. Abbas's position."

The *Times'* August 7, 2014 editorial says that:

Prime Minister Benjamin Netanyahu of Israel, has signaled an eagerness to have [the PA] extend its reach to Gaza. But it cannot just be a policeman. If any agreements come out of [impending ceasefire negotiations in] Cairo, they must be designed to strengthen the authority and its president, Mahmoud Abbas, by managing whatever funds are donated to Gaza. It may be necessary to have Hamas in Cairo but the group offers Palestinians nothing, but nihilism and endless suffering.[126]

In this passage, the paper claims for itself, for Israel, and by extension for Israel's American sponsor, the right to determine who should govern and represent the Palestinians: the paper presumes that Israel has the right to determine that the PA should be in charge in Gaza and that any ceasefire should empower the PA and marginalize Hamas. That Palestinians elected Hamas in 2006 goes unmentioned. The fact that Abbas lacks a democratic mandate is not taken into consideration. Because the passage suggests that weakening Hamas and excluding them from negotiations is a necessary feature of achieving peace, the story being told here is that Hamas' "nihilism" is among the central reasons that Palestinians are suffering. Framing the Palestine-Israel issue in these terms enables the editors to say that for the Palestinians' own good their politics should be supervised by their oppressors.

Calls to ensure PA dominance within Palestinian politics are effectively endorsements of US-Israeli colonial management of the Palestinians because the PA is itself largely an articulation of US-Israel power. The PA was born out of the 1993 Oslo Accords, which, combined with a series of subsequent deals, are referred to as the Oslo peace process. The Israeli government and the Palestine Liberation Organization (PLO) signed these agreements, which were supposed to involve Israel's phased withdrawal from the occupied West Bank and Gaza so as to generate the good faith needed to resolve, in final status negotiations, the issues of Palestinian refugees' right to return, Israel's settlements, the status of Jerusalem, and where the borders would be. To speak of the PA is to speak of Oslo and vice-versa. Tariq Dana writes that the PA's existence is "fully dependent on" the accords and notes that the agreements were:

> implemented against the backdrop of the expansion of global capitalism which requires, by consent or coercion, conforming dynamics and trends to facilitate the engineering of neo-liberal consensus at the global scale. The globalisation of capitalism has introduced new forms of 'peace processes' that are largely based on economic incentives and compromises, thus contributing to the formation of a locally influential political-economic elite that is tied into the global system economically, ideologically and politically....[T]he Oslo process and, by extension, the later myriad rounds of the Palestinian-Israeli peace talks should be placed within an understanding of the global dynamic.[127]

Since its inception, the PA has been part of an effort to consolidate and expand US-led capitalism across the globe. US hegemony in the region and beyond "is codified in its dominance over the Oslo process," which created policies ostensibly pursued in the name of "peace" that heavily involved international donors and international financial institutions in "designing and conditioning the very structure and policies of the nascent PA."[128] For example, between 1994 and 2001, multilateral, bilateral, transnational, national, governmental, and nongovernmental organizations invested close[129] to $3 billion in various projects undertaken in the name of the "peace process."[130] In the years that followed, the neoliberal policies promoted by these international bodies have guided the PA's own economic planning.[131] International donors have supported Palestinian elites that Israel regards as "partners for peace" who support the "peace process" while marginalizing other Palestinian elites.[132] By contrast, funds such as those provided by the United States Agency for International Development (USAID) cannot legally go to groups that the American government considers terrorist organizations such as Hamas, Islamic Jihad, or the leftist Popular Front for the Liberation of Palestine. In these ways, the PA has been from the beginning, at least partially, a conduit for global capitalist interests at the center of which is the American ruling class. Since 2007, when a Palestinian split left Hamas in charge of Gaza and the PA overseeing the West Bank, over 80 percent of aid from international donors to Palestinians has gone toward budget support for the PA.[133]

In a context where the US is the world's sole superpower, thanks in part to its Israeli client, the PA and the Oslo Accords from which it emerged have helped entrench Israeli domination of the Palestinians. This imbalance is evident in the way that management of the West Bank was divided into three sections. Area A, which is 2-3 percent of the West Bank, was placed under nominal PA control. Area B, comprising roughly 26 percent of the territory, was shared by Israel and the PA. The PA had civil and police powers while Israel was in charge of "internal security" and was allowed to define this term. Area C, which included 70 percent of the West Bank, was completely under Israeli control. Mouin Rabbani shows that when, as per Oslo, the Israeli military was redeployed from much of the West Bank and Gaza, "Israeli control over Palestinians was exercised with greater vigor than at any time since the occupation began in June 1967."[134] The Palestinian towns in Area A are non-contiguous and Israel retained management of the roads connecting them and therefore "all movement of goods and persons into and out of, and between, these enclaves could be and was interdicted at will."[135] In Area B, the Oslo Accords enabled Israel to carry out "land confiscations, mass arrests, house demolitions, defoliation, prolonged curfews, [and] arbitrary violence." Area C surrounds Areas A and B and was not subject to restrictions on the expansion of Israeli settlements. It includes border regions, main roads, and the water-rich areas of the West Bank. This process left Palestinians "penned up in disconnected fragments of occupied territory encircled by ever-expanding settlements."[136]

Similarly, the political fruits of western and Israeli backing of the PA can be seen in such instances as when, in the face of protests from Palestinians, PA President Mahmoud Abbas decided that the PA would not push for the UN General Assembly to adopt the Goldstone Report, a document that enraged Israel by accusing both it and Hamas of committing war crimes during Israel's 2008-2009 war on Gaza.[137]

The PA has facilitated rather than impeded Israel's power over the Palestinians. For instance, one crucial function of the PA has been to help enforce Israeli "security." Western aid has been used to train and control PA security forces to protect the PA and Israel from Palestinian resistance but not to protect the Palestinian population from external threats such as Israel.[138] Thus the PA has repressed its Palestinian political opponents, often in close coordination with the Israeli state. Rabbani concludes that the bulk of the violence PA security forces inflicted on Palestinians was "aimed at improving the [PA's] standing with Israel and the West."[139] When the US began its 2001 bombing and Afghanistan, 1,000 Palestinians, many and them students, undertook a protest beginning at Islamic University in Gaza. Palestinian police in riot gear were waiting just 500 meters from the campus and the students threw rocks at the police while the police fired tear gas and live ammunition and three were killed in riots that broke out across Gaza.[140] The PA has undertaken other campaigns of repression in, for example, Jenin refugee camp in 2007, 2008, and 2013.[141]

There is also a revolving door between the PA's prisons and Israel's.[142] For example, in 2006 Israel captured Popular Front for the Liberation of Palestine Leader Ahmad Sa'adat from a PA jail, where his incarceration was overseen by British and American guards.[143] Israeli-PA security cooperation is also an expression of US power as these efforts have been overseen by the Office of the US Security Coordinator.[144] PA-US ties are so deep that Abbas has even advocated a US-led NATO occupation of Palestine.[145]

The economic arrangements to which the PA agreed during Oslo further evince that the group has facilitated Israeli control over the Palestinians. One agreement signed during the Oslo process was the 1994 Paris Economic Protocols (PEP), which gave the PA superficial economic power and allowed Israel to retain control of key features of the economy such as borders, land, natural resources, labour, freedom of movement, trade, fiscal management, industrial zoning, and water resources.[146] Israeli products typically had unrestricted entry to Gaza while "Israel's policy on Palestinian exports sought to ensure continued dependence upon Israel and prevent the emergence of an autonomous Palestinian economy."[147] Most Palestinians became poorer after Oslo.[148] Under the accords, Palestinian construction is only allowed in 1 percent of Area C of the West Bank, which is an especially serious problem because it is the logical place for the large infrastructure projects necessary to build a self-sufficient society such as waste-water treatment plants, waster pipelines, and main roads.[149]

Israel and the PA have also partnered in industrial projects in which Israel is the dominant party. These ventures, the most notable of which are four joint export-oriented industrial zones, were sponsored by international donors, require Israeli authoriz-ation, and give Israeli capital a foothold in the West Bank.[150] By prioritizing investors' rights while limiting Palestinian workers' rights, the zones allow for the super-exploitation of Palestinian labour.[151] Such initiatives, furthermore, take place in the context of Israel's overall control of Palestinian resources, infrastructure, lands, borders, and of the movement of people and goods inside the West Bank.[152] Dana finds that the joint economic ventures demonstrate that "capitalist interaction between the coloniser and colonised has come to constitute a mechanism of control that serves colonial entrenchment and pacification" by perpetu-ating Israeli occupation and settler-colonialism and seeking to "ensure the domestication of the [Palestinian] population and their acceptance of the status quo."[153]

Pacification has also taken place by creating a Palestinian middle class dependent on the PA and the Oslo process. By 2013, 160,000 Palestinians in the West Bank and 42,000 of them in Gaza were employed in the PA's public service. Therefore, as Mandy Turner points out, a large section of the population is tied into the PA's stability and future existence.[154] Since Oslo, moreover, Israel has reduced its reliance on Palestinian labour in areas like construction and agriculture by replacing many of these workers with migrant labour from regions such as Asia and Eastern Europe, meaning that employment by the PA has become a key means of survival for Palestinians.[155] Furthermore, Turner notes, Oslo has empowered a section of the Palestinian political and business elite who have a vested interest in the "peace process," operating as they do "in an economic context structured by the occupation, the PEP, and the Oslo peace paradigm," which makes them dependent upon having good relations with the Israeli government and Israeli businesses.[156]

Another sense in which Oslo can be seen as a pacification project is that it has led to NGOs unaccountable to Palestinians coming to play a major role in administering Palestinian society. The reason Palestinians consistently require substantial international aid is that they lack sovereignty over their own natural and human resources, which Israel controls.[157] As Rema Hammami and Salim Tamari argue, in the initial phases of the Second Intifada "professionalized" NGOs were among the few structures available to organize civil resistance and "their structural limitations (professional organizations lacking a mass base) and programmatic emphasis on developmental and governance issues have made them incapable of organizing at the mass level."[158] Hammami and Tamari's research, for example, indicates that Oslo and the PA's state formation process "profoundly" hindered the capacity of the Palestinian population to engage in popular mobilization during the early stages of the uprising.[159]

The Oslo process aligned with post-Cold War US interests as President George H.W. Bush and President Clinton calculated that "the US-Israeli strategic alliance must accommodate a certain role for Arab partners" such as Jordan, whose King Hussein supported Oslo, and that "Arab-Israeli peace was consistent with maintaining a Middle Eastern Pax Americana."[160] Since the PA colludes in this process, media demands that the PA be strengthened can be understood as demands that US-managed Israeli domination of Palestinians be further entrenched.

CHAPTER THREE: ISRAEL DOES NOT HAVE A RIGHT TO DEFEND ITSELF

News media outlets frequently present outbreaks of large scale violence in Palestine-Israel in terms of "Israel's right to defend itself." This narrative says that whatever Israel may be guilty of, the state is justified in using military force to respond to Palestinian attacks. Framing Palestine-Israel in terms of Israeli security conceals how Israel initiates the vast majority of violent exchanges with the Palestinians. Media narratives about "Israel's right to defend itself," moreover, mislead readers by ignoring the permanent violence of Israel's colonization of Palestine and the aggressive pursuit of ethnic supremacy that this colonization entails.

For example, a June 7, 2014 *New York Times* editorial on the Palestinian unity deal, the collapse of which helped precipitate that summer's war, suggests that Israeli Prime Minister Benjamin Netanyahu had good reason to say that Israel would not negotiate with a Palestinian government that includes Hamas.[1] The editors write that Hamas is "committed to Israel's destruction. Gaza militants regularly fire rockets into Israel; in 2012, Hamas fought an eight-day war with Israel." This sentence suggest that Hamas has no right to engage in a war with Israel, even when Israel initiates it, as was the case in the 2012 fighting. In contrast, the sentence implies that Israel does have a right to carry out a war against Hamas and the rest of the Palestinians affected by such actions. The *Times* goes on to describe Hamas' "heavily armed militia" as a barrier to resolving the Palestine-Israel question but makes no similar comment about Israel's vastly more powerful military arsenal, which includes nuclear weapons. In this editorial, the legitimacy of the colonizer's violence is unquestioned whereas the violence of the colonized is presented as illegitimate.

Similarly, the *Times'* July 19, 2014 editorial says that Israel "sent tanks and ground troops into Gaza to keep Hamas from pummeling Israeli cities with rockets and carrying out terrorist attacks via underground tunnels."[2] In this passage, the editors unquestioningly amplify Israel's rationale for its ground incursion into Gaza. Israel, in this conception, is merely defending itself from Hamas' violence, even though Israel initiated that summer's fighting and even though the UN[3] would later find that "during the period under examination, the tunnels were only used to conduct attacks directed at IDF positions in Israel in the vicinity of the Green Line, which are legitimate military targets". The editors then write:

> There was no way Prime Minister Benjamin Netanya-
> hu was going to tolerate the Hamas bombardments,

which are indiscriminately lobbed at Israeli population centers. Nor should he. As President Obama said on Friday, "No nation should accept rockets being fired into its borders, or terrorists tunneling into its territory." Well over 1,000 rockets have fallen on Israel since July 8, and they have reached farther than ever, threatening Tel Aviv and beyond. Only two Israelis have died (a civilian was killed by mortar shells from Gaza as he distributed food to soldiers near the border on Tuesday, and an Israeli soldier may have been killed by friendly fire at the start of the ground offensive), but Israeli citizens are running for cover from incoming rockets.

The phrase "nor should he" is an explicit endorsement of Israel's war on the Strip premised upon the argument, put forth by Netanyahu and Obama, that Israel is simply exercising its right to defend itself from Hamas' attacks. This narrative is furthered by the portions of the article that suggest Hamas's violence is severe both because of its volume, which is emphasized in the reference to "1,000 rockets," and because of the scope of its effects, which apparently reach "farther than ever, threatening Tel Aviv and beyond" so that "Israeli citizens are running for cover from incoming rockets." These aspects of the article suggest that Hamas' actions are so dangerous to Israel that the latter is justified in using the massive military operation that it has undertaken and presumably has no alternative but to do so. Similarly, the editors write that "Hamas can't defeat Israelis, so it tries to terrorize them." According to this framing, Hamas rockets "terrorize" Israelis, thus rendering the group's political aims illegitimate, but the Israeli invasion and bombardment of Gaza does not "terrorize" Palestinians. Implicitly, this argument suggests that Israel's violence is used for the just purpose of protecting Israelis.

The *Times'* July 25, 2014 editorial on Protective Edge asserts that "Surely, Israel has reason to take strong military action against the barrage of rockets on its territory and to destroy Hamas's underground tunnels." In none of the paper's editorials on Protective Edge are the Palestinians afforded a right "to take strong military action" to defend themselves from Israeli airstrikes and ground troops or to end the siege of Gaza or to achieve any other aim. The editors tell readers that Hamas is "committed to Israel's destruction," which reinforces the idea that Israel has no choice but to unleash an intense military onslaught against anyone presumed to belong to the group or anyone who is in their vicinity.

In the paper's August 7, 2014 editorial, the *Times* argues that impending talks between Israelis and Palestinians with Egyptian mediation need to go beyond establishing a ceasefire to halt the fighting taking place that summer and to address problems underlying the violence. The editors, however, write that in order for that to happen:

> Certain conditions are clear. Rocket attacks into Israel by Hamas and other extremist groups must stop, along with other terrorist attacks. So does the smuggling of weapons into Gaza and the production of a new supply of rockets. There will need to be an international donors' conference to rebuild Gaza, but with assurances that Hamas will not divert money for civilian projects into rockets and tunnels. Otherwise, there is little chance that Israel would end the blockade that has kept Gazans confined to the strip, and deprived them of imports, exports and jobs.

By saying that Palestinian militants must be stopped from engaging in violence and denied the means to do so and making no such claims about Israel, this excerpt suggests that the conduct of Hamas and its allies is the root cause of the 2014 war. The story being told here is one of an innocent Israeli state under attack.

The *Times'* account of the tunnels is misleading. When the editors say that Hamas should be prevented from using money for civilian projects on tunnels, the paper is overlooking the extent to which the tunnels are, in addition to having military purposes, also a civilian project. The tunnels are the "driver of Gaza's economy" and the partnerships that funded initial tunnel construction "encompassed a cross section of Gaza society" as capital for them was raised through mosque networks.[4] Farmers used the tunnels to circumvent Israel's ban on seeds, pesticides, irrigation pipes, and agricultural tools such as hoes and buckets; the cheaper inputs enabled by the tunnels helped factories resume operations; a food-processing plant started working again because items banned by Israel such as preservatives, plastic wrapping, and spare parts arrived from Switzerland via tunnel.[5] After 2008-2009's Operation Cast Lead, the tunnels enabled Gaza's residents to re-build the territory themselves. The UN projected that, given the comprehensiveness of Israel's blockade, it would take Palestinians 80 years to re-build the 6,000 housing units destroyed in Cast Lead without the tunnels and only 5 years with them.[6] The productivity of the tunnels has ebbed and flowed and they are a less reliable method of economic activity than the above-ground importing and exporting that would take place if Israel lifted the blockade. Yet in endorsing the destruction of the tunnels, the *Times*' editors are calling for one of the few lifelines that besieged Gaza residents have to be severed. Here "Israel's right to defend itself" translates into Israel's right to further undermine Palestinians' capacity to develop agriculture, have factories, process food, and rebuild after Israeli wars against them.

The conditions these passages outline for ending the 2014 war and preventing another one consist of multiple demands of

Palestinians and no demands of Israelis. In this regard, the editors are implying that Israel has the right to continue carrying out violence against Palestinians and denying them basic rights such as the freedom to move and engage in economic activity, all of which apparently falls under the rubric of Israeli self-defence, until the Palestinians meet Israeli demands. Unless that happens, readers are told, "there is little chance that Israel would end the blockade." Here the editors describe the Israeli violence that takes the form of the blockade in neutral language and without any insistence that it end, whereas Palestinians "must" refrain from using force or securing the capacity to use force. Israel's bombardment and invasion of Gaza is thereby treated as natural and legitimate. Thus, this passage is an example of the problem with framing Palestine-Israel in terms of "Israel's right to defend itself" in that it prioritizes Israeli safety over the safety or rights of Palestinians.

INITIATING VIOLENCE

The Israeli security narrative rests on the dubious assumption that keeping its citizens safe is the preponderant priority of the Israeli state. If it were, Israel would not consistently take actions that undermine ceasefires and negotiations. Yet it has a long-term history of doing precisely that. During an October 2000 pause in the Second Intifada, Israel sabotaged a ceasefire with Arafat by continuing its policy of extra-judicially assassinating Palestinian activists.[7] The state went on to kill the Popular Front for the Liberation of Palestine's West Bank political leader Abu 'Ali Mustafa and Fatah leader Thabit Thabit, who was actively engaged in ceasefire discussions with Israel.[8] On July 24, 2002 Fatah signed an agreement for a unilateral ceasefire, which Hamas was on the verge of accepting, until Israel killed Hamas founder Salah Shihadah and 14 of his friends, family members, and neighbors.[9] According to an analysis by three academics from the US and Israel, during the Second Intifada of 2000-2005, 79% of all pauses in the violence ended when Israel killed a Palestinian, while only 8% were interrupted by Palestinian attacks.[10] The authors find that this pattern is more pronounced during longer conflict pauses in that "of the 25 periods of nonviolence lasting longer than a week, Israel unilaterally interrupted 24, or 96%, and it unilaterally interrupted 100% of the 14 periods of nonviolence lasting longer than 9 days."[11]

This pattern has persisted in the major military operations that Israel has undertaken in Gaza since its 2005 re-deployment from the territory and since Hamas' victory in the January 2006 elections. On June 8th 2006, Israel carried out a targeted assassination that killed Jamal Abu Samhadana, a senior Hamas security official, and three others.[12] Following that attack, Palestinian militants responded by shooting rockets at Israel, which caused no casualties, and Israel launched an airstrike that hit a family beach picnic in Gaza and killed seven, including three children.[13] A June 13th Israeli airstrike killed 11 Palestinians, nine of them civilians, two of them paramedics, and two of them children.[14] A week later, an Israeli strike on Gaza's Jabaliya refugee camp killed three Palestinians, a girl aged 6 and two boys, one aged 5 and the other aged 16. In the first twenty days of that month, Palestinians fired more than 140 rockets from Gaza, seriously hurting one person and slightly injuring several others.[15] On June 24th, Israeli soldiers entered Gaza and captured two brothers, Osama and Mustafa Abu Muamar, who Israel said were Hamas members, though Hamas denied this.[16] The next day two Palestinian militants crossed the border into Israel via a tunnel and captured the Israeli soldier Gilad Shalit. Two Palestinians and two Israeli soldiers were killed in the incident. The Palestinians holding Shalit said they would release him if Israel released the roughly 95 Palestinian women and 313 Palestinians under 18 in Israeli jails.[17] On June 28th, Israel began a military incursion into Gaza and on the 30th it began bombing the territory. Israel called its mission Operation Summer Rains, which led to Operation Autumn Clouds, and this round ended on November 26th.

Six months prior to 2008-2009's Operation Cast Lead, Israeli Defense Minister Ehud Barak instructed the Israeli military to prepare for the attack even as the state was negotiating a ceasefire with Hamas,[18] which suggests bad faith on Israel's part. A ceasefire was reached and lasted approximately six months until Israel violated it on November 4th by raiding a residential area in Gaza, killing a senior Hamas commander and two other members of the group.[19] Hamas responded by firing ten mortars at Israel that caused no damage, injuries, or death, and Israel then carried out airstrikes that killed 5 more Hamas members and tightened its siege to a nearly total closure of Gaza. After that, Palestinians fired rockets at Israel.[20]

Israel's 2012 operation Pillar of Defense provides a similar example. The violence began when Israeli soldiers fatally shot 13-year-old Ahmad Abu Daqqa while he was playing football outside his house in Gaza; Palestinian militants retaliated by attacking an Israeli armored personnel carrier, which injured several Israeli soldiers.[21] Israel then shelled another football field and a mourning tent, killing four civilians and wounding dozens, while four Israelis were hurt by subsequent missiles that Palestinians fired.[22] The war started just as an agreement for a permanent ceasefire between Israel and Hamas was being put together. Israel instead opted to assassinate Hamas military chief Ahmed al-Jabari, who had been part of the negotiations and was expected to agree to the deal: veteran Israeli military analyst Reuven Pedatzur points out that Israel assassinated the man who had the power to make a deal with them and asks, "If they knew it was possible to reach a cease-fire agreement (whose provisions, incidentally, were better [for Israel] than those of the agreement reached after the operation) without going to war, why did they assassinate Jabari, and thereby also assassinate the chances of achieving calm without shooting?"[23] For the last five and a half years of his life, Jabari had ensured that Gaza's armed groups observed truces with Israel and had worked with the state to negotiate the release of the captive Israeli soldier Gilad Shalit and to ensure his well-being, which led the editor-in-chief of the Israeli paper *Haaretz* to describe Jabari as "a subcontractor, in charge of maintaining Israel's security in Gaza."[24] According to Pedatzur, Jabari's assassination "signaled to Hamas that communications with it will be conducted only through military force."[25] If Israel wanted to protect its citizens, as the "self-defence" narrative claims, it could have had a long-term cessation of violence with the Palestinians even without reaching a comprehensive settlement with them. Instead, it opted to kill Jabari and carry out a war.

The lead up to 2014's operation Protective Edge illustrates a similar flaw in the "self-defence" frame. Hamas, cash-starved and short on strong allies outside of Palestine, agreed to an accord "on terms set almost entirely by . . . Palestinian Authority president, Mahmoud Abbas" that created a government that gave the PA a foothold in Gaza, was formed without a single Hamas member, and contained Abbas' prime minister, deputy prime ministers, finance minister and foreign minister.[26] The new Palestinian government pledged to abide by the principles set out by the Middle East Quartet (the UN, US, EU, and Russia), which include recognizing Israel, rejecting violence, and abiding by existing agreements involving Israel and the Palestinians.[27] Nathan Thrall writes that Israel:

> immediately sought to undermine the reconciliation agreement by preventing Hamas leaders and Gaza residents from obtaining the two most essential benefits of the deal: the payment of salaries to 43,000 civil servants who worked for the Hamas government and continue to administer Gaza under the new one, and the easing of the suffocating border closures imposed by Israel and Egypt that bar most Gazans' passage to the outside world.

The United States and its European allies also helped undermine the deal. When Qatar offered to pay the salaries of the civil servants, the US government said that American law prohibited any entity delivering payment to those employees, even though thousands of them are not even members of Hamas, because they are all considered by American law to have received material support from a terrorist organization. The Obama administration then failed to assist when a UN envoy offered to deliver the salaries through the United Nations so as to exclude all parties from legal liability.[28] If Israel needed to protect its citizens from Hamas, as the "self-defence" narrative takes for granted, then Israel would have encouraged a unity deal that marginalized Hamas in favor of the PA and saw it commit to non-violence and recognition of Israel.

Moreover, in the period leading up to Protective Edge, Israel frequently violated the ceasefire it had agreed to with Palestinian armed groups in Gaza following Israel's November 2012 Operation Pillar of Defense. Data compiled by Visualizing Palestine indicates that, between the November 22nd, 2012 truce and July 7th, 2014, Israel committed 191 ceasefire violations and Palestinians carried out 75 violations; 10% of Israel's breaches resulted in death as did 4% of the Palestinians'.[29]

The "Israeli self-defence" frame presupposes that Israel has no choice but to use military force to protect its citizens; On the contrary, Israel has consistently violated ceasefires and it has repeatedly killed Palestinian interlocutors capable of and often willing to deliver ceasefire deals. Israel has chosen to start wars against a population it oppresses and, in that respect, the Israeli "self-defence" narrative is a fictional one.

MASS KILLINGS

The Israeli state was founded by massacring and ethnically cleansing Palestinians. Since Israel was created, it has repeatedly massacred Palestinians and Arabs in other countries, notably Lebanon. That Israel has frequently and deliberately killed scores of civilians and endured nothing comparable in scale demonstrates that narratives about "Israel's right to defend itself" are untenable.

On the nights of October 14th and 15th in 1953, the Israeli military killed between 60[30]-70[31] Palestinian villagers in Qibya. The operation in Qibya followed a Palestinian attack in the Israeli Yehud settlement that killed a woman and two of her children. The people killed in Qibya had no connection to the killings in Yehud.[32] The Central Command of the Israeli military received orders from Israeli political leaders including Prime Minister David Ben-Gurion to "carry out destruction and maximum killing with the aim of driving the inhabitants of the village from their homes."[33] In Qibya, Israeli forces went door-to-door "throwing grenades through the windows, and 'cleaning out' the rooms with light weapons fire. Inhabitants who tried to flee their homes were gunned down in the alleyways.[34] Subsequently, Israeli paratroops blew up forty-five of the village's houses; most of the victims in Qibya were women and children.[35]

In October 1956, the Israeli army shot 48 Palestinian labourers in Kafr Kassim, a town on the armistice line between the West Bank and the Israeli state. The victims were on their way home from work when they "were lined up and summarily shot for unknowingly 'violating' a curfew that had been announced only thirty minutes earlier.[36] In 1956 Israel briefly occupied Gaza, which was then under Egyptian control, prior to and throughout the Suez Crisis in which Israel, Britain, and France attacked Egypt. During that period Israeli forces carried out two mass killings. On November 3rd 1956, Israeli forces killed 275 civilians at Khan Yunis and a nearby refugee camp and then nine days later killed 111 more civilians at Rafah refugee camp.[37] A mass grave uncovered in Khan Yunis held the corpses of forty Arabs who had been shot in the back of the head after their hands had been tied.[38]

Israel, moreover, bears responsibility for the 1982 slaughter of more than two thousand unarmed Palestinian and Lebanese civilians in the Sabra and Shatila refugee camps that was carried out by right-wing Lebanese militias allied with Israel. At the time of the killing, Rashid Khalidi points out, "these camps were under Israeli military control, in a city occupied by the Israeli army, and were lit overnight by Israeli army flares as the butchers went about their work."[39] The slaughter, according to Pappe, was "encouraged and incited by Israeli military officers of the highest rank."[40]

In December 1987, the Palestinians began a mass uprising, the First Intifada, that lasted until the signing of the Oslo Accords on September 13th 1993. In that timeframe, Israeli security forces killed 1,113 Palestinians, 237 of them under the age of 17, and Israeli civilians and settlers killed 75 more Palestinians, 13 of them children.[41] By contrast, Palestinians killed 60 people who were in Israel's security forces and 100 Israelis who were not, 5 of whom where minors.[42] Israelis, in short, killed ten times more Palestinians than Palestinians killed Israelis. These killings are also qualitatively different in that Palestinian violence was a consequence of their being denied self-determination for four decades and Israeli violence was part of their effort to keep Palestinians from exercising that right.

During the 2000-2005 Second Intifada, 950 Israelis were killed by Palestinians: 83 Israeli security forces and 418 Israeli civilians were killed in Israel and 436 Israelis were killed in the West Bank and Gaza, half of whom were security forces.[43] Even during the Second Intifada, however, far more Palestinians were killed by Israelis than vice-versa. 3,169 Palestinians were killed by Israelis in the West Bank and Gaza and 54 Palestinians were killed in Israel by Israeli security forces; a further 34 Palestinians were killed by Israeli civilians and settlers and of the total number of dead Palestinians, 631 were less than 18 years old while 112 of the Israeli fatalities were under 18.[44] In the period, therefore, nearly three and a half times as many Palestinians were killed by Israel as Israelis were killed by Palestinians. Moreover, one year into the intifada, an Amnesty International report criticized Palestinian violence against Israeli civilians, including suicide bombings, but the document reveals the massive difference in the scale of Israeli and Palestinian violence of that period when it notes:

> All Palestinians in the Occupied Territories — more than three million people — have been collectively punished. Almost every Palestinian town and village has been cut off by Israeli army checkpoints or physical barriers. Curfews on Palestinian areas have trapped residents in their homes for days, weeks or even months. In the name of security, hundreds of Palestinian homes have been demolished.[45]

While thousands of Israeli civilians were harmed during the intifada, virtually every Palestinian in the West Bank, Gaza, and East Jerusalem was repressed and controlled. There is also a qualitative difference in the violence that occurred between 2000-2005 in that Palestinians were expressing discontent at how the Oslo Accords had deepened rather than alleviated Israeli control over their lives and to more than half a century of colonization and repression by the Israeli state whereas Israeli violence was a continuation and intensification of those conditions.

In the 1990s and 2000s, as in the 1980s, not only Palestinians but also Lebanese people endured Israel violence. Israel occupied Lebanon from 1982-2000, inflicting grave harm on Lebanese and Palestinians in that period and after. In 1996, the Lebanese group Hezbollah launched rockets into Israel in retaliation for the killing of Lebanese civilians and, after the rocket fire, Israel launched Operation Grapes of Wrath in Lebanon in a failed effort to undermine Hezbollah's popular support in Lebanon and to compel Syria to rein in the organization.[46] No Israeli civilians died in this operation whereas Israel killed approximately 154 Lebanese civilians.[47] During Grapes of Wrath, Israel massacred 106 civilians at the UN base in Qana, a protected zone under international law. The victims were seeking safety from Israeli air and ground attacks but they were killed when Israel deliberately shelled the UN building.[48] Over the course of Israel's 18 year occupation of Lebanon, Israel's day-to-day "shoot first and ask questions later" policy, led to the deaths of more than 500 Lebanese and Palestinian civilians, more than 30 times the number of Israeli civilians killed during this time.[49] In July 2006, Hezbollah captured two Israeli soldiers in what the group's leader Shaykh Hassan Nasrallah said was a response to the siege that Israel, the US, and Europe had imposed on Gaza in January of that year following Hamas' victory in the Palestinian election.[50] Israel then launched a war in which roughly 1,200 Lebanese people were killed, including hundreds of children, while 43 Israeli civilians died.[51] Around one million people in Lebanon were displaced by Israeli attacks, which destroyed tens of thousands of homes and a great deal civilian infrastructure.[52]

More recent fighting in Gaza has seen Israel initiate violence against the Palestinians they were occupying, colonizing, and subjecting to a siege and then killing Palestinians at a rate far higher than Palestinians killed Israelis.[53] During Israel's June-November 2006 Operation Summer Rains and Operation Autumn Clouds, 416 Palestinians and 5 Israelis were killed, one of them by friendly fire.[54] Israel's attack damaged Gaza's only power plant and, the UN reports, "seriously hampered the functioning of health facilities, water wells, sewage disposal facilities and access to water in buildings of Gaza City."[55] During the operation the Strip was "totally devastated"[56] and Israel closed Gaza's borders, causing thousands of people to either be trapped inside or outside of the Strip, many of them returning home from medical treatment abroad via the Rafah crossing at the Egyptian border: 6 Palestinians, including 3 children, died as they were left at the Rafah crossing.[57] According to John Dugard, the UN's Special Rapporteur for human rights in the

Palestinian Territories, Israeli actions violated international humanitarian and human rights law.[58] He said that in Gaza people were without water, food was scarce, and medicine was running out, and that Israel's siege violated the prohibition of collective punishment.[59] Moreover, Dugard said that it contravened the prohibition against "measures of intimidation and terrorism" contained in the Fourth Geneva Convention and that the arrest of Hamas Cabinet ministers and legislators appeared to constitute the "taking of hostages" barred by the convention.[60]

In December 2008-January 2009, Israel carried out Operation Cast Lead in Gaza.[61] Human Rights Watch reports that in areas densely populated with civilians Israel illegally used white phosphorous, which causes intense burns to the skin, can seriously damage internal organs, and can cause death.[62] Amnesty International criticized Palestinian rocket fire but the harm caused by the rocket fire does not begin to approach that of Israeli attacks which, in Amnesty's words, "violated fundamental provisions of international humanitarian law, notably the prohibition on direct attacks on civilians and civilian objects (the principle of distinction), the prohibition on indiscriminate or disproportionate attacks, and the prohibition on collective punishment."[63] Palestinians' use of force, moreover, is qualitatively different from Israel's in that Palestinian violence is that of a people reacting to a flare-up of violence initiated by the state that is occupying and besieging them. During Cast Lead, Israel killed approximately 1,391 Palestinians in Gaza, around 759 of whom were civilians, whereas Palestinians killed 6 members of the Israeli security forces and 3 civilians.[64] Israelis killed 344 Palestinian minors in Gaza and Palestinians killed zero Israeli minors.[65]

Similarly, Israel carried out Operation Pillar of Defense in Gaza in November 2012. Between January 2012 and when the November fighting began, Israeli fire killed 78 Palestinians whereas Hamas' rocket fire killed 1 Israeli.[66] PCHR finds evidence that Israeli war crimes were widespread during Pillar of Defense.[67] While Human Rights Watch criticizes Palestinian armed groups for indiscriminate rocket fire, Palestinian actions were not nearly as destructive as Israel's. Israeli military attacks "struck civilians and civilian objects, such as houses and farm groves, without any apparent military objective," including one that killed three men in a truck carrying tomatoes, one that killed a science teacher who was sitting outside with his 3-year-old son on his lap; other Israeli attacks killed a 79-year-old man and his 14-year-old granddaughter in the family's olive grove, a farmer and his nephew as they were walking on a road near their olive trees, and a 28-year-old woman carrying a blanket in her yard.[68] Palestinian violence, moreover, is qualitatively different from Israel's in that Palestinian rocket fire is against a state that ethnically cleansed, blockaded and occupied them and initiated this round of fighting. Over the course of Pillar of Defense at least 168 Palestinians were killed by the Israeli military, 101 of them believed to be civilians, including 33 children, while 4 Israeli civilians, none of them children, and 2 members of their security forces died.[69]

It's the same story in each round of violent escalation in Gaza since 2006: Israel initiates fighting by killing Palestinians it has oppressed for nearly seven decades and, when the Palestinians eventually respond, Israel uses the response to kill hundreds of Palestinian civilians, more than a thousand in the cases of Cast Lead and Protective Edge, and faces an extremely small number of its own civilian casualties. Yet a cross-section of media outlets replace that story with one about "Israel defending itself."

These killings, from Qibya to Protective Edge, are some of the more egregious instances of killings Israel has carried out against Palestinians but this list is far from a comprehensive documentation of all such cases. What these examples illustrate is that news media outlets are not telling an accurate story when they frame Palestine-Israel in terms of "Israel's right to defend itself." The state cannot be seen as defending itself when it has carried out the most frequent and most deadly killings in the history of its relations with Palestinians and Arabs in neighbouring countries.

ISRAELI SELF-DEFENCE IS A LOGICAL IMPOSSIBILITY

The untenable narrative that describes Israel's use of force as a just form of "self-defence" against the threat of Palestinian violence elides the ways in which the entire Zionist project, which long predates the existence of Israel as a state, has involved violently subjugating the Palestinians. Avi Shlaim finds that "violence was implicit in Zionism from the beginning, that the Arab-Israeli conflict was an inescapable consequence of the Zionist program" because "Zionism sought to create a Jewish state in a land that was already inhabited by another people."[70] His research indicates that "since the 1920s the Zionist movement has had a clear strategy for dealing with the Arabs— the strategy of relying on military power in order to achieve its political ends," which is known as "the strategy of the iron wall."[71] Because the Israeli state and its forerunners in the Zionist movement have pursued their aims through the perpetual use of violence against Palestinians, Palestinians by definition cannot initiate violence and Israel. That means that the idea of "Israeli self-defense" is a logical impossibility.

Darryl Li, similarly, describes the Zionist enterprise as "the creation, maintenance, with (when possible) the expansion of a state for the Jewish people" that, when it is faced with opposition from the indigenous non-Jewish population, "produces a well-known longstanding operational mantra guiding Zionist settlement and annexation policies: maximum land, minimum Arabs. When circumstances prohibit Israel from pushing natives beyond the territory it controls, this dictum produces a corollary: maximum Arabs on minimum land."[72] Joseph Massad points out that, throughout its history, Zionism has remained unashamed about "its commitment to building a demographically exclusive Jewish state modeled after Christian Europe, a notion pervaded . . . by a religio-racial epistemology of supremacy over the Palestinian Arabs."[73] For instance, he notes that "It is a commitment to Jewish supremacy that makes the return of Palestinian refugees a "demographic threat" to the Jewish majority of Israel (which became a fact precisely because the Palestinians now seeking to return to their lands and homes were expelled from them in the first place)."[74] As Steven Salaita writes, "The Palestinian who welcomes the opportunity to share a nation and a national identity with Jews exposes the irreconcilable contradiction of Zionism, that something called a "Jewish state" can also be a legitimate democracy."[75]

Pursuing the largest possible amount of land and the fewest possible number of Arabs has entailed forcibly taking Palestinian land while separating the Palestinians from each other and preventing them from having a viable, independent society. The 1967 Allon Plan, for example, called for Israeli annexation of 25-40 percent of the West Bank, including Jerusalem and its immediate surroundings, a territory 10–15 kilometers wide along the Jordan Rift Valley, and the Judean Desert.[76] The plan would separate East Jerusalem and the West Bank as well as the northern from the southern West Bank in order to preserve Israeli control over the Jordan Valley and Dead Sea, to provide Israel with a strategic buffer, and to prevent the emergence of an independent Palestinian state.[77] Although Israel never officially adopted the plan, it "defined the framework for Israeli land control" by establishing the concept of security borders, which Israel used to justify land confiscations, and "reasserted the importance of building Israeli settlements as a way of ensuring the incorporation of the maximum amount of land with the fewest number of Palestinians."[78]

Israeli policy in Jerusalem is also indicative of the state's demographic priorities. In 1970 Israel began creating a "Greater Jerusalem" by redrawing the boundaries of the city to include Jewish-only settlements and by restricting the natural growth of Arab neighborhoods in East Jerusalem.[79] Three years later the Israeli state legally mandated a 73-26 demographic advantage for Jewish people in Jerusalem.[80] Much of the Palestinian housing construction that takes place in East Jerusalem violates Israeli law. It is prohibitively difficult for an Arab to get a building permit because these are very expensive and because they are not granted in areas with infrastructure shortages, which is an

Israeli-created problem in many Palestinian neighborhoods.[81] Because these Palestinian homes are deemed illegal, Israel has a pretext for demolishing them. It is seriously misleading to cast a state that bulldozes houses and takes land at gun point as acting in self-defence against the people being dispossessed.

In Jerusalem, differential legal rights help minimize the presence of Arabs. Salim Tamari describes how Palestinian Jerusalemites are given blue ID cards, providing them "residency rights but not citizenship rights. Their status was suspended in limbo. Palestinians in the outer periphery, outside the greater Jerusalem area were given green IDs, which blocked them from entry to the city." Since the Israeli state classifies East Jerusalem as part of the country, residents of the West Bank and Gaza Strip require a permit from the Israeli military authorities to enter the city that had long been the center of Palestinian cultural and economic life.[82] Yet Palestinian birth rates have driven the Arab population of Jerusalem so the state and the municipality pressures Palestinians to leave the city. Andy Clarno writes that

> efforts to quietly transfer Palestinians out of Jerusalem have been standard for over thirty years. These efforts have intensified since the early-1990s, when Israel began aggressively confiscating the Jerusalem identity cards of Palestinians who could not prove that Jerusalem was

the 'center of their life.' Unless Palestinian Jerusalemites could provide evidence that they both lived and worked in Jerusalem, the Ministry of the Interior confiscated their Jerusalem residency documents and forced them to relocate to other parts of the West Bank.[83]

Because Israel considers Jerusalem part of the country, it has undertaken these policies to simultaneously maximize the amount of territory under its control while keeping the number of Palestinians living there as small as possible.

Israel's separation wall is a further tool of securing demographic superiority for Jewish Israelis in Jerusalem. When or if the wall is completed, it "will exclude several Arab neighborhoods from Jerusalem. This is the case of Samiramis, Kafr Aqab, Shu'fat refugee camp, Ras Khamis, Dahiyat As Salam, and Al Walaja. These neighborhoods are inhabited by almost 55,000 Arab Jerusalemites."[84] The Kafr Aqab and Shu'fat refugee camps are two of the most densely populated Palestinian neighbourhoods in Jerusalem.[85] That Israel has used a militarized wall to appropriate land and engineer a demographic majority is lost, however, in narratives about the state's "right to defend itself."

On the West Bank, vast areas have been effectively annexed to Israel through the wall and through the expansion of settlements and their infrastructure so that now Palestinians cannot access a near majority of West Bank lands for residential or economic use.[86] Such walls are built, Li explains, because

> Israel's notion of "security" is inherently expansive: security of the Jewish population demands that Arab movement be controlled and that Arabs be kept away from Jews. Securing this arrangement requires putting those Arabs behind a wall. And such a wall in turn demands its own protection. The ideal way to secure a barrier is through a vacant "buffer zone."

In Gaza, creating buffer zones has meant forcibly emptying the spaces in which they have been created of Palestinians, their houses, and their agriculture: for example, during the Second Intifada Israel razed 1,600 homes in Rafah.[87] A similar process has occurred in the "seam zone" between the Green Line and the separation barrier. A 2003 Israeli military order in the West Bank declared the northern seam zone a "closed military area" off-limits to virtually all Palestinian non-residents while requiring that the roughly 5,000 Palestinians who are residents apply to the military every six months to have the right to stay in their homes while Jewish people of any nationality have free access to the area.[88]

During the Second Intifada, Israeli housing demolitions in Gaza left at least 21,000 Palestinians homeless. According to Sara

Roy, this period saw an intensification of Israel's closure policy as well as the destruction of physical resources—such as homes, businesses, public buildings, factories, electricity infrastructure, vehicles, roads, schools, clinics, waste disposal and sanitation systems, water supply networks, telecommunications equipment, and agriculture, land, crops and infrastructure—all of which depleted Palestinians' capital stock and immobilized the population, leaving the Palestinians' economy dramatically eroded and their access to work, food, housing and other necessities severely undermined.[89] In these ways, Israeli violence against Palestinians is manifest not only in its immediate physical impact on Palestinian persons but in its consequences for their capacity to have a society in which they develop an economy and social services. Furthermore, Roy points out that both the re-deployment from Gaza and the Oslo process serve Israel's goals of maintaining "full control—both direct and indirect—over all Palestinian lands and resources; . . . securing, to the extent possible, demographic separation with the Palestinians, and thereby guaranteeing a Jewish majority within Israel . . . and insuring that if a Palestinian state is declared, it will be weak, diminished, and highly dependent on Israel."[90]

Moreover, military sieges of the sort imposed on Gaza are acts of war. In 2006, when Hamas won the Palestinian elections, a senior Israeli official said that Israel's planned response "is to put the Palestinians on a diet, but not to make them die of hunger."[91] Israeli health officials calculated the minimum number of calories needed by Gaza's 1.5 million inhabitants to avoid malnutrition and translated them into the number of truckloads of food Israel was supposed to allow in each day.[92] They said Israel should allow 170 trucks per day but only an average of 67 per day entered compared to over 400 trucks before the blockade was enacted.[93] Christian Cardon, the head of the Red Cross' Gaza office, said in April 2014 that Gazans face one of the highest unemployment rates in the world, "poverty, chronic fuel shortages and a scarcity of materials and equipment, which adversely affects health, water, sanitation, and electricity infrastructures."[94] Cardon added that "in 2013 the Gazan gross domestic product fell by around 3 per cent and is still below 1990s levels. In fact, the real average daily wage was lower in 2013 than it was in the 1990s." He noted that "the limits on the importation of affordable medical necessities . . . have created additional medium and long-term strain on an already fragile healthcare system. Many medical items, drugs and disposables have decreased in availability by up to 35 per cent since June 2013." Thus Cardon said that "The pervasive restrictions on the movement of people for medical, educational and economic purposes should be eased." Because the blockade is enforced militarily, Israel is effectively making war against Palestinians as long as the blockade is in place. Thus the

Palestinians cannot be said to be initiating violence while they are being besieged and no action Israel takes against Palestinians can be understood as defensive as long as a siege is in place.

These salient features of Palestine-Israel demonstrate that narratives about Israel exercising its legitimate "right to defend itself" are misguided. In effect every aspect of Israeli policy toward Palestinians is undergirded by violence or its threat. The record above indicates that a more accurate version of the story of Palestine-Israel would describe how the Palestinians have been violently colonized. Yet nothing in my research indicates that conventional British and American media want their audiences to think of the Palestinians as people, families, and communities with a right to defend themselves.

CONCLUSION

To understand why western news outlets proffer narratives about Palestine-Israel that favour Israel, it is necessary to consider these media outlets' political function. Joseph Uscinski explains that, "There is no doubt that systemic economic forces such as the need to sell advertising space and manage expenditures, determine the actions of news firms."[1] Multiple studies support the notion that the commercial orientation of news media shapes its content. An early 1990s academic survey of editors at daily newspapers finds that just under ninety percent reported that advertisers attempted to influence the content of stories appearing in their papers and ninety percent of them had advertisers apply economic pressure to them because of their reporting; 37 percent admit to capitulating to advertiser pressure.[2] Another academic survey of daily newspapers, this one published in 2007, finds that there are "frequent conflicts between the business side and the journalism side of newspaper operations" and that "advertising directors are willing to appease their advertisers, and are also willing to positively respond to advertisers' requests."[3] The survey suggests that this problem is particularly acute at chain-owned newspapers, which are especially prone to compromising editorial integrity to either please their advertisers or keep from offending them.[4] A similar problem exists in television, where polls of network news correspondents say that nearly one third feel directly pressured to report certain stories and not others because of owners' or advertisers' financial concerns.[5]

When coverage of Palestine-Israel is viewed in the context of commercial media, it is no surprise that narratives about the issue that are favourable to Israel are as prevalent as they are. The outlets covering Palestine-Israel are embedded in a system of global imperialist capitalism built around U.S hegemony of which Israel is an important characteristic. The overall functioning of the international capitalist system of which the commercial media are a part is guaranteed by the US military and, as I have shown in Chapter Two, American sponsorship of Israeli settler-colonial capitalism is a key part of US planners' strategy for dominance of the Middle East. The millionaire and billionaire owners of media outlets and of the advertisers that fund them are unambiguously part of the ruling class. The same is true, at least in the case of major national or international news organizations, of editors and often, as Hirji points out, journalists themselves who "belong to a societal elite" and "contribute, however, unconsciously to reinforcing existing notions about the way the world is."[6] One could add that such ideological administration also involves shaping beliefs about how the world should be and is capable of being. The stories of Palestine-Israel examined in these pages suggest that elites involved in the news making process believe that the violent oppression of Palestinians and the permanent consigning of them to the status of refugees and stateless persons is no great injustice, and that American stewardship of the Middle East is necessary and desirable.

The Palestine-Israel narratives discussed throughout this book are case studies in the harmful effects of the capitalist character of news media. Uscinski describes the commercial orientation of news media as a "market failure" with a significant "negative externalit[y]." "Low-quality news," he writes, "provides a low-quality information environment for democratic decision-making."[7] The three widespread narratives about Palestine-Israel discussed throughout this book are, as I have shown, highly misleading. An accurate rendering of the story would tell of Israel violently colonizing Palestine, with vital US support, and functioning as a garrison for US-led imperialist capitalism. Instead news media outlets present fables in which both Israelis and Palestinians have subjected each other to comparable wrongs and are blame-worthy to a similar extent for the unresolved status of Palestine. Readers are also offered disorienting accounts saying that the problem is that extremists are driving events in Palestine-Israel rather than moderates. Equally unhelpful are the tales the news tells about Israel's supposed "right to defend itself." Providing the public with such "low-quality information" about the issue distorts "democratic decision-making" by decreasing the likelihood of portions of the populations of America and other western countries substantial enough to compel policy changes coming to recognize that their governments' support for Israeli settler-colonial capitalism has devastating consequences for the Palestinians and proliferates war in the Middle East. As Entman writes, "framing appears to be a central power in the democratic process, for political elites control the framing of issues. These frames can determine just what "public opinion" is."[8]

The social role of commercially-oriented media, by which I mean news organizations that exist to make a profit and even those that do not but seek advertising revenue, is to advance ruling class interests. The western media is managed by the western ruling class and tells stories that steer the public toward attitudes favourable to that ruling class. As Hirji explains, "If there is a dominant narrative about a particular story or group, that narrative is likely informed by power relations: who has it, who does not have it, who wants to keep the status quo."[9] Such dominant narratives include perspectives on Palestine-Israel amenable to a situation wherein the US ensures that Israel remains the dominant military power in the region because that benefits US political and economic objectives. Stories hospitable to the ruling class proliferate in a media climate characterized by a "commercial system . . . [that] favours content that serves commercial interests. Markets favour speech that favours markets."[10] As Entman argues, moreover, framing "plays a major role in the exertion of political power, and the frame in a news text is really the imprint of power—it registers the identity of actors or interests that competed to dominate the text."[11] The way in which an issue is framed and the stories that arise from that framing have to be considered in the context of elite ownership over western media. That the western ruling class controls the media in their society and is deeply invested in Israeli settler-colonial capitalism but has no comparable interests in Palestinian liberation is crucial to grasping why western news outlets circulate narratives favourable to Israel. The people in charge of these outlets do not necessarily hatch conscious plots to trick the population into believing misleading tales about Palestine-Israel. The institutional orientation of news organizations steers them toward consistently framing issues in ways beneficial to the class to which they belong whether the topic is Palestine-Israel or any number of other subjects.

For the question of Palestine to be resolved, the western ruling class will have to be prevented from backing Israel as a means of dominating the Middle East. Because of western military, financial, and political support for Israel, public opinion in western societies has a role to play in brining a just, de-colonial peace across historic Palestine. Western states will not undertake the massive policy shifts necessary for that to happen unless mass pressure compels them to do so. Yet the structure of western news media suggests it is unlikely to begin telling stories about Palestine-Israel that are less weighted in Israel's favour, which means that this formidable barrier to building the popular sentiments necessary to stop western imperialism will remain in place for the foreseeable future. The task of bringing about the necessary shifts in consciousness therefore falls to independent news outlets and publishers as well as the activists working within and beyond them on campuses, in workplaces, in religious communities, and on the streets. This work is proliferating and the gains that the BDS movement has won in each of these realms attest to that. Such achievements demonstrate that getting the public in western countries to understand that the ruling class under which we live has been a key player in doing grave injustice to Palestinians, and that this is one key component in a system of global inequalities this class oversees, is a major challenge but not an insurmountable one.

ENDNOTES

INTRODUCTION

1. Robert Entman. "Framing: Toward a Clarification of a Fractured Paradigm." *Journal of Communication* 43.4 (Autumn 1993): 51-8.
2. Joseph N. Cappella and Kathleen Hall Jamieson. *Spiral of Cynicism*. (NY: Oxford UP, 1997). 39-40.
3. Entman 54.
4. Faiza Hirji. "The Colour of Difference: Race, Diverstiy, and Journalism in Canada." *Mediascapes: New Patterns in Canadian Communication*. Ed. Leslie Regan Shade. Fourth Edition. (Toronto: Nelson, 2014.) 395.
5. Cappella and Jamieson 42.
6. Nahla Abdo. "Women, War, and Peace: Reflection From the Intifada." *Women's Studies International Forum* 25.5 (2002): 587-88.

CHAPTER ONE: NOT "BOTH SIDES"

1. Gaza: Two Years Since The 2014 Hostilities," *United Nations Office for the Coordination of Humanitarian Affairs*, 30 August 2016, < https://www.ochaopt.org/content/gaza-two-years-2014-hostilities-august-2016>.
2. "50 Days: More Than 500 Children," *B'Tselem*, <http://www.btselem.org/2014_gaza_conflict/en/il/>.

3. Nathan Thrall. "How the West Chose War in Gaza." *New York Times* 17 July 2014: A23.

4. Thrall A23.

5. "Four Horrific Killings," editorial, *The New York Times* 8 July 2014.

6. Sara C Nelson. "Unarmed Palestinian Teens 'Shot Dead By Israeli Troops': UN Demands Investigation," *Huffington Post*, 21 May 2014, <http://www.huffingtonpost.co.uk/2014/05/21/unarmed-palestinian-teens-shot-dead-israeli-troops-un-demands-investigation_n_5363300.html>

7. "Israeli forces shoot and kill two Palestinian teens near Ramallah," *Defense for Children International*, 17 May 2014, <http://www.dci-palestine.org/israeli_forces_shoot_and_kill_two_palestinian_teens_near_ramallah>

8. "Israel's War in Gaza," editorial, *The New York Times* 19 July 2014.

9. "Making the Gaza Cease-Fire Last," editorial, *The New York Times* 7 August 2014.

10. "Palestine/Israel: Indiscriminate Palestinian Rocket Attacks," *Human Rights Watch*, 9 July 2014 <https://www.hrw.org/news/2014/07/09/palestine/israel-indiscriminate-palestinian-rocket-attacks>

11. "Protection of Civilians Weekly Report 10-16 June 2014," *United Nations Office for the Coordination of Humanitarian Affairs*, 19 June 2014, <https://www.ochaopt.org/content/protection-civilians-weekly-report-10-16-june-2014>.

12. U.N Relief and Works Agency, "*OPT Emergency Appeal Report 2013*," 30 April 2014, <https://www.unrwa.org/resources/reports/opt-emergency-appeal-report-2013>. 11

13. Lisa Hajjar, "Is Gaza Occupied and Why Does it Matter?" *Jadaliyya*, 14 July 2014, <http://www.jadaliyya.com/pages/index/8807/is-gaza-still-occupied-and-why-does-it-matter>.

14. U.N. Relief and Works Agency. The United Nations Country Team (UNCT) in the occupied Palestinian territory (oPt), "*Gaza in 2020:*

A Livable Place?" August 2012, 16 <https://www.unrwa.org/user-files/file/publications/gaza/Gaza%20in%202020.pdf>

15. "The Scope of Israeli Control in the Gaza Strip," *B'Tselem*, 5 January 2014, http://www.btselem.org/gaza_strip/gaza_status

16. Noura Erakat, Rashid Khalidi, and Mouin Rabbani. "FAQ on Failed Effort to Arrange a Ceasefire Between Israel and Hamas," *Jadaliyya* 16 July 2014. <http://www.jadaliyya.com/pages/index/18577/faq-on-failed-effort-to-arrange-ceasefire-between->

17. "Israel-Hamas Peace Agreement Text," *Huffington Post*, 21 November 2012. http://www.huffingtonpost.com/2012/11/21/israel-hamas-peace-agreement-text_n_2171602.html.

18. Noura Erakat, Rashid Khalidi, and Mouin Rabbani. "FAQ on Failed Effort to Arrange a Ceasefire Between Israel and Hamas." *Jadaliyya* 16 July 2014. <http://www.jadaliyya.com/pages/index/18577/faq-on-failed-effort-to-arrange-ceasefire-between->

19. "Israel's War in Gaza," editorial, *The New York Times* 19 July 2014.

20. "Occupied Palestinian Territory: Gaza Emergency Situation Report as of 17 July 2014, 1500 hrs)." *United Nations Office for the Coordination of Humanitarian Affairs* 18 July 2014 <https://www.ochaopt.org/content/occupied-palestinian-territory-gaza-emergency-situation-report-17-july-2014-1500-hrs>

21. "Gaza's Mounting Death Toll," editorial, *The New York Times* 25 July 2014.

22. "Occupied Palestinian Territory: Gaza Emergency Situation Report (as of 24 July 2014, 1500 hrs)," *United Nations Office for the Coordination of Humanitarian Affairs*, 25 July 2014, <https://www.ochaopt.org/content/occupied-palestinian-territory-gaza-emergency-situation-report-24-july-2014-1500-hrs>.

23. "Occupied Palestinian Territory: Gaza Emergency Situation Report (as of 24 July 2014, 1500 hrs)," *United Nations Office for the Coordination of Humanitarian Affairs*, 25 July 2014, <https://www.ochaopt.

org/content/occupied-palestinian-territory-gaza-emergency-situation-report-24-july-2014-1500-hrs>.

24. "Israel/Gaza: Attacks on medical facilities and civilians add to war crime allegations," *Amnesty International*, 21 July 2014, <https://www.amnesty.org/en/latest/news/2014/07/israelgaza-attacks-medical-facilities-and-civilians-add-war-crime-allegations/>.

25. "Gaza: Israel Must Stop Bombing Civilians," *Doctors Without Borders*, 20 July 2014, <http://www.doctorswithoutborders.org/news-stories/press-release/gaza-israel-must-stop-bombing-trapped-civilians>.

26. "Another Bloody Day of the Israeli Offensive on Gaza: Dozens Palestinian Civilians Killed or Wounded by Israeli Attacks in Khuza'a, 'Abassan and al-Qarara Villages; Israeli Forces Attack Gaza from the Air, the Sea and the Ground; More Palestinians Forcibly," *Palestine Centre for Human Rights*, 24 July 2014. <http://pchrgaza.org/en/?p=1612>.

27. "Another Bloody Day of the Israeli Offensive on Gaza: Dozens Palestinian Civilians Killed or Wounded by Israeli Attacks in Khuza'a, 'Abassan and al-Qarara Villages; Israeli Forces Attack Gaza from the Air, the Sea and the Ground; More Palestinians Forcibly," *Palestine Centre for Human Rights*, 24 July 2014. <http://pchrgaza.org/en/?p=1612>.

28. "Another Bloody Day of the Israeli Offensive on Gaza: Dozens Palestinian Civilians Killed or Wounded by Israeli Attacks in Khuza'a, 'Abassan and al-Qarara Villages; Israeli Forces Attack Gaza from the Air, the Sea and the Ground; More Palestinians Forcibly," *Palestine Centre for Human Rights*, 24 July 2014. <http://pchrgaza.org/en/?p=1612>.

29. Occupied Palestinian Territory: Gaza Emergency Situation Report (as of 23 July 2014, 1500 hrs)," United Nations Office for the Coordination of Humanitarian Affairs, 25 July 2014, <https://www.ochaopt.org/content/occupied-palestinian-territory-gaza-emergency-situation-report-23-july-2014-1500-hrs>.

30. "Occupied Palestinian Territory: Gaza Emergency Situation Report (as of 24 July 2014, 1500 hrs)," *United Nations Office for the Coordination of Humanitarian Affairs*, 25 July 2014, <https://www.ochaopt.org/content/occupied-palestinian-territory-gaza-emergency-situation-report-24-july-2014-1500-hrs>.

31. "On the 27th Day of the Israeli Offensive:Rafah Under Israeli Fire; War Crimes Committed against Palestinian Civilians; Complete Families Annihilated," *Palestine Centre for Human Rights*, 3 August 2014. <http://pchrgaza.org/en/?p=1603>.

32. "Israel-Palestine"—Glimmers of Sanity Amid the Tragic Killings," editorial, *The Observer* 6 July 2014: OB 32.

33. Jonathan Freedland. "Israel's Fears are Real but This War is Utterly Self-Defeating." *The Guardian* 26 July 2014: GRDN 41.

34. Michael Cohen. "Is the Arab-Israeli Conflict Going to be the War That Never Ends?" *The Observer* 3 August 2014: OB 32.

35. Sally Kohn. "Why I'm Against Hamas, Against What Israel Is Doing, and For Judaism," *Daily Beast*, 25 July 2014. <http://www.thedailybeast.com/articles/2014/07/25/why-i-m-against-hamas-against-what-israel-is-doing-and-for-judaism.html>

36. James Bloodworth. "The Middle East Debate Has More to Do With the Fashion for Revolutionary Tourism Than Real Politics," *The Independent*, 14 July 2014. <http://www.independent.co.uk/voices/comment/arguments-about-israel-and-palestine-have-more-to-do-with-the-fashion-for-revolutionary-tourism-than-9604934.html>

37. Will Gore. "When Both Palestinians and Israelis Think We are Biased, We Must Be Doing Something Right," *The Independent*, 13 July 2014. <http://www.independent.co.uk/voices/comment/when-both-palestinians-and-israelis-think-we-are-biased-we-must-be-doing-something-right-9603068.html>

38. "Four Horrific Killings," editorial, *The New York Times* 8 July 2014.

39. Dean Obeidallah. "How John Stewart Made it Okay to Care About Palestinian Suffering," *Daily Beast*, 7 July 2014. <http://www.thedailybeast.com/articles/2014/07/21/how-jon-stewart-made-it-okay-to-care-about-palestinian-suffering.html>.

40. Ali A. Rizvi. "7 Things to Consider Before Choosing Sides in the Middle East Conflict," *Huffington Post*, 28 July 2014. < http://www.huffingtonpost.com/ali-a-rizvi/picking-a-side-in-Israel-Israel_b_5602701.html>.

41. H.A Goodman. "It's Immoral for Hamas to Use Human Shields and Immoral for Israel to Bomb Human Shields," *Huffington Post*, <http://www.huffingtonpost.com/h-a-goodman/its-immoral-for-hamas-to_b_5629548.html>.

42. Lisa Taraki. "Even-Handedness and the Palestinian-Israeli/Israeli-Palestinian "Conflict."" *Contemporary Sociology* 35.5 (Sept 2006): 449.

43. Ilan Pappe. *The Ethnic Cleansing of Palestine*. (London: Oneworld Publications, 2006) xiii and 15.

44. Ibrahim Abu-Lughod. "Territorially-Based Nationalism and the Politics of Negation." *Blaming the Victims* Ed. Edward Said and Christopher Hitchens. (London: Verson, 1988) 201.

45. Emphasis in original. Rashid Khalidi. *The Iron Cage*. (Boston: Beacon, 2006) 33.

46. Edward Said. *The Question of Palestine*. (New York: Vintage, 1992) 98.

47. Pappe *The Ethnic Cleansing of Palestine* 14.

48. Pappe *The Ethnic Cleansing of Palestine* 14.

49. Pappe *The Ethnic Cleansing of Palestine* 14.

50. Pappe *The Ethnic Cleansing of Palestine* 14.

51. Pappe *The Ethnic Cleansing of Palestine* 34-5.

52. Pappe *The Ethnic Cleansing of Palestine* 30-5.

53. Pappe, *The Ethnic Cleansing of Palestine* 40.

54. Pappe, *The Ethnic Cleansing of Palestine* xiii and 8-9

55. Rashid Khalidi, *The Iron Cage* 131.

56. Pappe *The Ethnic Cleansing of Palestine* 58.

57. Pappe *The Ethnic Cleansing of Palestine* 59.

58. Nur Masalha. "The Palestinian Nakba: Zionism, 'Transfer' and the 1948 Exodus." *Global Dialogue* 4.3 (Summer 2002): 84.

59. Rashid Khalidi *The Iron Cage* 133.

60. Masalha, "The Palestinian Nakba" 85.

61. Masalha, "The Palestinian Nakba" 87-8.

62. Masalha, "The Palestinian Nakba" 88.

63. Edward Said, *The Question of Palestine* 98-9.

64. Rashid Khalidi, *The Iron Cage* 136.

65. "In Figures," *United Nations Relief and Works Agency*, January 2014, <https://www.unrwa.org/sites/default/files/2014_01_uif_-_english.pdf>.

66. "BADIL is proud to announce the release of its biennial Survey of Palestinian Refugees and Internally Displaced Persons 2010–2012," *BADIL*, <http://www.badil.org/en/press-releases/142-2012/3638-press-eng-53?pid=20>.

67. Ilan Pappe. *A History of Modern Palestine*. (Cambridge: Cambridge UP, 2004) 187.

68. Rashid Khalidi. *Sowing Crisis*. (Boston: Beacon, 2009) 208.

69. Ilan Pappe. *A History of Modern Palestine* 188.

70. Rashid Khalidi. *Sowing Crisis* 128.

71. United Nations, General Assembly. *Situation of Human Rights in the Palestinian Territories Occupied Since 1967*. A/65/331 (30 August 2010), available from <https://unispal.un.org/DPA/DPR/unispal.nsf/eed216406b50bf6485256ce10072f637/69bec99af727e-ac2852577c3004aad8a?OpenDocument>.

72. "Annual Report: Israel and the Occupied Palestinian Territories 2013," *Amnesty International*, 23 May 2013, <http://www.amnestyusa.org/research/reports/annual-report-israel-and-the-occupied-palestinian-territories-2013?page=show>.

73. United Nations Office for the Coordination of Humanitarian Affairs Occupied Palestinian Territories. *West Bank Movement and Access Update.* (May 2009), available from <https://unispal.un.org/DPA/DPR/UNISPAL.NSF/9a798adbf322aff38525617b006d88d7/b3edbb76dafddd6a852575c20065e305?OpenDocument>.

74. United Nations, General Assembly. *Situation of Human Rights in the Palestinian Territories Occupied Since 1967.*

75. "Separate and Unequal," *Human Rights Watch.* 19 December 2010. <https://www.hrw.org/report/2010/12/19/separate-and-unequal/israels-discriminatory-treatment-palestinians-occupied>.

76. United Nations Human Rights Council. "*Report of the Special Rapporteur on the Situation of Human Rights in the Palestinian Territories Occupied Since 1967, John Dugard.*" A/HRC/4/17 (29 January 2007), available from < https://documents-dds-ny.un.org/doc/UNDOC/GEN/G07/105/44/PDF/G0710544.pdf?OpenElement>. 16.

77. United Nations Human Rights Council. "*Report of the Special Rapporteur on the Situation of Human Rights in the Palestinian Territories Occupied Since 1967, John Dugard.*" 16

78. United Nations Human Rights Council. "*Report of the Special Rapporteur on the Situation of Human Rights in the Palestinian Territories Occupied Since 1967, John Dugard.*" 17.

79. United Nations Office for the Coordination of Humanitarian Affairs Occupied Palestinian Territories. "*The Humanitarian Impact of Gaza's Electricity and Fuel Crisis.*" (March 2014), available from <https://www.ochaopt.org/documents/ocha_opt_electricity_factsheet_march_2014_english.pdf >.

80. United Nations Office for the Coordination of Humanitarian Affairs Occupied Palestinian Territories. "*The Humanitarian Impact of Gaza's Electricity and Fuel Crisis.*"

81. United Nations Environment Program. "*Environmental Assessment of the Gaza Strip.*" (September 2009). <https://unispal.un.org/pdfs/DEP_1190_GE.pdf>. 6

82. U.N. Relief and Works Agency. The United Nations Country Team (UNCT) in the occupied Palestinian territory (oPt), *"Gaza in 2020: A Livable Place?"* 5

83. "Discriminatory Water Supply," *B'Tselem*, 27 September 2016. <http://www.btselem.org/water/discrimination_in_water_supply>.

84. "Water for One People Only," *Al-Haq*, 2013. <http://www.alhaq.org/publications/Water-For-One-People-Only.pdf>. 16.

85. "Discriminatory Water Supply," *B'Tselem*.

86. "Statistics." *Addameer*, May 2014. <http://www.addameer.org/statistics/20140501>.

87. "Administrative Detention." *B'Tselem*, 21 September 2014. <http://www.btselem.org/administrative_detention>.

88. "Statistics." *Addameer*, January 2017. <http://www.addameer.org/statistics/20170131>.

89. United Nations Commission on Human Rights. *"Civil and Political Rights, Including the Questions of: Torture and Detention."* E/CN.4/2002/NGO/162 (20 February 2002), available from <https://unispal.un.org/DPA/DPR/unispal.nsf/0/E5DFDA7A80736E-C185256B89005BC22C>

90. Administrative Detention," *B'Tselem*, <http://www.btselem.org/administrative-detention-old/administrative-detention>

91. "Statistics," Addameer, May 2014, <http://www.addameer.org/statistics/20140501>

92. "Settler Violence: Lack of Accountability," *B'Tselem*, 1 January 2011. <http://www.btselem.org/settler_violence/dual_legal_system>.

93. "Joint input to the ENP Country Report on Israel 2013 Human rights of prisoners and detainees held in Israel, with focus on Torture / CIDT1." *Adalah, Al Mezan Centre for Human Rights, Physicians for Human Rights-Israel, Public Committee Against Torture in Israel*, October 2013, <https://www.adalah.org/uploads/oldfiles/Public/files/English/International_Advocacy/ENP/Joint-input-Prisoners-ENP-Israel-Oct-2013.pdf>. 1.

94. "Joint input to the ENP Country Report on Israel 2013" 1.
95. "Jewish National Fund Law," *Adalah*, <https://www.adalah.org/en/law/view/531>.
96. Rabab Abdulhadi, "Imagining Justice and Peace in the Age of Empire," *Peace Review* 16.1 (March 2004): 87.
97. "Ban on Family Unification," *Adalah*, <https://www.adalah.org/en/law/view/511>.
98. "Nakba Law," *Adalah*, <https://www.adalah.org/en/law/view/496>.
99. "Anti-Boycott Law," *Adalah*, <https://www.adalah.org/en/law/view/492>.
100. "On the 40th anniversary of Land Day: Adalah releases new report on Israel's discriminatory land and housing policies in 2015," *Adalah*, 30 March 2016, <https://www.adalah.org/en/content/view/8771>.
101. "Arab Minority Rights," *The Association for Civil Rights in Israel*, <http://www.acri.org.il/en/category/arab-citizens-of-israel/arab-minority-rights/>.
102. In its editorial on July 25th, the *Times* vaguely refers to the unity government but only to say that "Perversely" Protective Edge benefited Hamas's political leader, Khaled Meshal, because the group went from being politically weak before the war to "being hailed among Palestinians in the West Bank as a champion" without mentioning that its weakness led to a unity deal that Israel, the US, and Europe scuttled or that this was a major cause of the 2014 fighting.
103. Noura Erakat, Rashid Khalidi, and Mouin Rabbani.
104. Gershon Baskin. "What Israel Must Do Now," *Slate*, 10 August 2014. <http://www.slate.com/articles/news_and_politics/foreigners/2014/08/gaza_war_continues_here_s_what_israel_needs_to_do_to_hurt_hamas_and_help.html>.
105. "Israel, Hamas and the Rockets; The Level of Civilian Deaths in Gaza is unacceptable," editorial, *Financial Times*, 23 July 2014: FTFT USA Ed 1 06.

106. Joel Beinin and Rebecca L. Stein. "Histories and Futures of a Failed Peace." *The Struggle for Sovereignty* Eds. Joel Beinin and Rebecca L. Stein. (Stanford, CA: Stanford UP, 2006) 4

107. Rashid Khalidi. *Brokers of Deceit*. (Boston: Beacon, 2013) 57-8.

108. "20 Facts: 20 Years Since the Oslo Accords," *Oxfam*, 13 September 2013, available at <https://www.oxfam.org/en/pressroom/pressreleases/2013-09-13/20-years-missed-opportunity-has-undermined-progress-israel>.

109. Linda Tabar, "From Third World Internationalism to 'The Internationals': The Transformation of Solidarity with Palestine," *Third World Quarterly* 38.2 (2017): 414-35.

110. Pappe. *A History of Modern Palestine* 265.

111. Khalidi *Brokers of Deceit* 89.

112. Khalidi *Brokers of Deceit* 92-3.

113. Khalidi *Brokers of Deceit* 97.

114. Khalidi *Brokers of Deceit* 101.

115. Ali Abunimah, "Obama "Peace" Envoy Ridicules Notion That Palestinians Have "Rights."" *Electronic Intifada*, 9 May 2014 <https://electronicintifada.net/blogs/ali-abunimah/obama-peace-envoy-ridicules-notion-palestinians-have-rights>.

116. Jonathan Cook, "Peace Process is Doomed to Fail While Israel Stalls for Time," *The National*, 29 October 2013, <http://www.thenational.ae/thenationalconversation/comment/peace-process-is-doomed-to-fail-while-israel-stalls-for-time#full>.

117. Ori Lewis. "Israel Announces Plans for Building 1,400 Settlement Homes," *Reuters*, 10 January 2014, <http://www.reuters.com/article/us-palestinians-israel-settlements-idUSBREA090KW20140110>.017

118. "Israel Says Separation Wall Will Be Border," *Al-Jazeera*, 5 November 2013, <http://www.aljazeera.com/news/middleeast/2013/11/israel-says-separation-wall-will-be-border-201311514132609960.html>.

119. Taraki 450.

120. Abu-Lughod 205.

CHAPTER TWO: EXTREMISTS AND MODERATES

1. "Israeli-Palestinian Collision Course," editorial, *The New York Times* 7 June 2014.

2. United Nations, General Assembly, "Importance of the Universal Realization of the Right of Peoples to Self Determination and of the Speedy Granting of Independence to Colonial Countries and Peoples for the Effective Guarantee and Observance of Human Rights," A/RES/3246 (29 November 1974), available from <https://unispal.un.org/DPA/DPR/unispal.nsf/0/C867EE1DBF29A6E5852568C6006B2F0C>.

3. "Making the Gaza Cease-Fire Last," editorial, *The New York Times* 7 August 2014.

4. Mya Guarnieri, "What Does Israeli 'Acceptance' of Ceasefire Really Mean?" *+972 Magazine*, 15 July 2014, <https://972mag.com/what-does-israeli-acceptance-of-ceasefire-really-mean/93642/>.

5. Noura Erakat, Rashid Khalidi, and Mouin Rabbani.

6. Fares Akram, "Israel Threatens to Step Up Gaza Campaign," *Al-Jazeera*, 16 July 2014. <http://www.aljazeera.com/news/middleeast/2014/07/israeli-strikes-resume-after-brief-gaza-calm-201471511044177114.html>.

7. "Gaza's Mounting Death Toll," editorial, *The New York Times* 25 July 2014.

8. Anshel Pfeffer. "This is Not Just a Fight Over Land, It's a Religious War." *Guardian* 21 Nov 14: GRDN 45.

9. Sam Harris. "Why Don't I Criticize Israel?" *SamHarris.org*, 27 July 2014. <https://www.samharris.org/podcast/item/why-dont-i-criticize-israel>.

10. Rizvi.

11. "A Ceasefire for Gaza," editorial, *The Washington Post*, 30 July 2014.

12. Jeffrey Goldberg, "The Paranoid, Supremacist Roots of the Stabbing Intifada," *The Atlantic*, 16 Oct 2015. <https://www.theatlantic.com/international/archive/2015/10/the-roots-of-the-palestinian-uprising-against-israel/410944/>.

13. Nick Cohen, "Homophobia is Now Met With the Same Silence Given to Homophobia," *The Spectator*, 13 June 2016. <http://blogs.spectator.co.uk/2016/06/homophobic-murder-will-gays-become-new-jews/>.

14. Bloodworth.

15. Israel/Gaza Conflict: Questions and Answers," *Amnesty International*, 25 July 2014, <https://www.amnesty.org/en/latest/news/2014/07/israelgaza-conflict-questions-and-answers/>.

16 United Nations Human Rights Council, Report of the Detailed Findings of the Independent Commission of Inquiry Established Pursuant to Human Rights Council Resolution S-21/1, A/HRC/29/52 (22 June 2015), available from <http://www.ohchr.org/EN/HRBodies/HRC/CoIGazaConflict/Pages/ReportCoIGaza.aspx#report>. 91.

17. Joel Beinin. "The Oslo Process and the Limits of a Pax Americana." *The Struggle for Sovereignty* Eds. Joel Beinin and Rebecca L. Stein. (Stanford, CA: Stanford UP, 2006). 32.

18. Charmaine Seitz. "Coming of Age: Hamas's Rise to Prominence in the Post-Oslo Era." *The Struggle for Sovereignty* Eds. Joel Beinin and Rebecca L. Stein. (Stanford, CA: Stanford UP, 2006). 123.

19. Ali Abunimah, "What's Behind Hamas' New Charter?" Electronic Intifdada, 2 May 2017. <https://electronicintifada.net/blogs/ali-abunimah/whats-behind-hamas-new-charter>

20. Seitz 113.

21. Seitz 114-16.

22. Seitz 115-16.

23. Khaled Hroub. *Hamas: A Beginner's Guide*. 2nd ed. Ann Arbor, Mich: Pluto, 2010. X.

24. Beinin, "The Oslo Process and the Limits of a Pax Americana" 32.

25. Beinin, "The Oslo Process and the Limits of a Pax Americana," 32.

26. Seitz 115.

27. Beinin, "The Oslo Process and the Limits of a Pax Americana," 32.

28. Seitz 117.

29. Seitz 117.

30. Seitz 119.

31. Seitz 119.

32. Seitz 119.

33. Seitz 120.

34. Seitz 120.

35. Seitz 124.

36. Seitz 122.

37. Hroub XX.

38. Hroub XVIII.

39. Seitz 118.

40. Andrew Higgins, "How Israel Helped to Spawn Hamas," *Wall Street Journal*, Eastern Edition 24 January 2009: W1.

41. Seitz 127.

42. Seitz 127-8.

43. Pappe *A History of Modern Palestine* 248.

44. Pappe *A History of Modern Palestine* 248.

45. Pappe *A History of Modern Palestine* 249.

46. Pappe *A History of Modern Palestine* 249.

47. Pappe *A History of Modern Palestine* 249.

48. Hroub XX.

49. Hroub. *Hamas*. IX.

50. "Four Horrific Killings," editorial, *The New York Times* 8 July 2014.

51. Jonathan Freedland, "This Cycle of Vengeance Could Start a Third Intifada," *The Guardian*, 5 July 14: GRDN 33.

52. Noam Chomsky. *The Fateful Triangle*. (Montreal: Black Rose, 1984) 9.

53. Khalidi *Sowing Crisis* 17-8.

54. Khalidi *Sowing Crisis* 26.

55. Khalidi *Sowing Crisis* 27.

56. Chomsky *The Fateful Triangle* 21.

57. Khalidi *Sowing Crisis* 27.

58. Matthew Kelly, "US Middle East Policy and the State-Capital Controversy in Imperialism's Historiography." *Middle East Critique* 23.1 (2014): 83.

59. Khalidi *Sowing Crisis* 27.

60. Khalidi *Sowing Crisis* 28.

61. Khalidi *Sowing Crisis* 29.

62. Khalidi *Sowing Crisis* 29.

63. Khalidi *Sowing Crisis* 29.

64. Beinin. "The Oslo Process and the Limits of a Pax Americana." 22.

65. Chomsky *The Fateful Triangle* 21.

66. Adam Hanieh. ""Palestine in the Middle East: Opposing Neoliberalism and US Power Part 2." *MRonline*, 19 July 2008. <http://mrzine. monthlyreview.org/2008/hanieh190708b.html>.

67. Khalidi *Sowing Crisis* 145-8.

68. Khalidi *Sowing Crisis* 145-8.

69. Bashir Abu-Manneh, "Israel in the U.S Empire," *Monthly Review* 58.10 (March 2007), <http://monthlyreview.org/2007/03/01/israel-in-the-u-s-empire/>.

70. Abu-Manneh.

71. Chomsky *The Fateful Triangle* 22.

72. "Israel's Worldwide Role in Repression," *International Jewish Anti-Zionist Network*, 2012, <https://israelglobalrepression.files.wordpress.com/2012/12/israels-worldwide-role-in-repression-footnotes-finalized.pdf >.

73. Chomsky *The Fateful Triangle* 26.

74. Laleh Khalili, "The Location of Palestine in Global Counterinsurgencies." *International Journal of Middle East Studies* 42.3 (August 2010): 413-433.

75. Chomsky *Fateful Triangle* 21.

76. Chomsky *Fateful Triangle* 24-5.

77. Max Ajl, "The Biggest Israel Aid Deal in History Will Bolster Occu-
    pation and the U.S. Defense Industry," *In These Times*, 20 September
    2016. <http://inthesetimes.com/article/19479/the-israeli-aid-pack-
    age-10-more-years-of-the-special-relationship>.
78. Pappe *History of Modern Palestine* 208.
79. Khalili 418.
80. Khalili 420.
81. Khalili 416.
82. Khalili 416.
83. Khalili 418.
84. Khalili 420.
85. Khalili 418.
86. Berrigan, Frida. "Made in the U.S.A: American Military Aid to Israel."
    Journal of Palestine Studies 38.3 (Spring 2009): 9.
87. Berrigan 10.
88. Berrigan 18.
89. Ajl.
90. Berrigan 6.
91. Berrigan 9.
92. Ajl.
93. Hanieh "From State-Led Growth to Globalization: the Evolution of
    Israeli Capitalism," *Journal of Palestine Studies* 32.4 (Summer 2003):
    5-21.
94. Jonathan Nitzan and Shimshon Bichler. *The Global Political Economy
    of Israel.* (Lodon: Pluto, 2002) 16.
95. Hanieh "Evolution of Israeli Capitalism" 13.
96. David Cronin, "Warren Buffett Signs $2 Billion Check in Support
    of Israeli Apartheid," *Electronic Intifada*, 6 May 2013. <https://elec-
    tronicintifada.net/blogs/david-cronin/warren-buffett-signs-2-bil-
    lion-check-support-israeli-apartheid>.
97. Jewish Telegraphic Agency, "US Billionaire Warren Buffett
    Invests $5M in Israel Bonds, Helps Raise $60M." *Times of Israel*,

8 November 2016. <http://www.timesofisrael.com/us-billionaire-warren-buffett-invests-5m-in-israel-bonds-helps-raise-60m/>.

98. Inbal Orpaz, Amitai Ziv, Haim Bior, "TechNation Facebook to Hire 40 for New Tel Aviv Office," *Haaretz*, 24 March 2015, <http://www.haaretz.com/israel-news/business/tech-roundup/.premium-1.648485>.

99. "Our Locations," *Google Careers*, <https://careers.google.com/locations/>.

100. "HP Labs Israel Celebrates 20 Years of Innovation," *Hewlett Packard Enterprise Community*, 22 May 2014 <https://community.hpe.com/t5/Behind-the-scenes-Labs/HP-Labs-Israel-celebrates-20-years-of-innovation/ba-p/6793252#.WNrRK6K1vIU>.

101. David Shamah, "Tim Cook: Apple's Herzliya R&D Center Second-Largest in World," *Times of Israel*, 27 February 2015 <http://www.timesofisrael.com/apples-herzliya-rd-center-now-second-largest-in-world/>.

102. Hanieh "Palestine in the Middle East: Opposing Neoliberalism and US Power Part 2."

103. Hanieh "Palestine in the Middle East: Opposing Neoliberalism and US Power Part 2."

104. Hanieh "Palestine in the Middle East: Opposing Neoliberalism and US Power Part 2."

105. Hanieh "Palestine in the Middle East: Opposing Neoliberalism and US Power Part 2."

106. Hanieh "Palestine in the Middle East: Opposing Neoliberalism and US Power Part 2."

107. Seymour Hersh, "The Redirection," *The New Yorker*, 5 March 2007, <http://www.newyorker.com/magazine/2007/03/05/the-redirection>.

108. As'ad Abukhalil, "The Left and The Syria Debate," *Jadaliyya*, 10 December 2016, <http://www.jadaliyya.com/pages/index/25628/the-left-and-the-syria-debate>.

109. Hanieh "Evolution of Israeli Capitalism" 7.

110. Hanieh "Evolution of Israeli Capitalism" 8.

111. Beinin "The Oslo Process and the Limits of a Pax Americana" 23.

112. Hanieh "Evolution of Israeli Capitalism" 12.

113. Yoav Peled, "From Zionism to Capitalism," *The Struggle for Sovereignty* Eds. Joel Beinin and Rebecca L. Stein. (Stanford, CA: Stanford UP, 2006). 43.

114. Beinin "The Oslo Process and the Limits of a Pax Americana" 34.

115. Ajl.

116. Peled 52.

117. Joel Beinin, "Confronting Settlement Expansion in East Jerusalem," *Middle East Research and Information Project*, 14 February 2010, <http://www.merip.org/mero/mero021410>.

118. Salim Tamari, "The Future of Jerusalem: Sacred Space or Open City," *Institute for Palestine Studies*, 11 July 2011, <http://www.palestine-studies.org/institute/fellows/future-jerusalem-sacred-space-or-open-city>.

119. Adam Hanieh. "Palestine in the Middle East: Opposing Neoliberalism and US Power Part 1."

120. "Water for One People Only" 16.

121. Adam Hanieh. "Palestine in the Middle East: Opposing Neoliberalism and US Power Part 1."

122. *United Nations Office for the Coordination of Humanitarian Affairs Occupied Palestinian Territories West Bank Movement and Access Update* 6.

123. *Advisory Opinion Concerning Legal Consequences of the Construction of a Wall in the Occupied Palestinian Territory*, International Court of Justice (ICJ), 9 July 2004, available at <http://www.icj-cij.org/docket/index.php?pr=71&code=mwp&p1=3&p2=4&p3=6>.

124. "Israeli-Palestinian Collision Course," editorial, *The New York Times* 7 June 2014.

125. "Israel's War in Gaza," editorial, *The New York Times* 19 July 2014.

126. "Making the Gaza Cease-Fire Last," editorial, *The New York Times* 7 August 2014.

127. Tariq Dana. "The Symbiosis Between Palestinian 'Fayyadism' and Israeli 'Economic Peace': The Political Economy of Capitalist Peace in the Context of Colonisation." *Conflict, Security & Development* 15.5 (December 2015): 457.

128. Dana 461.

129. Mandy Turner. "The Political Economy of Western Aid." *Decolonizing Palestinian Political Economy*. Eds Mandy Turner and Omar Shweiki. (Hampshire: Palgrave, 2014). 39-40.

130. Rema Hammami and Salim Tamari. "The Second Uprising: End or New Beginning?" *Journal of Palestine Studies* 30.2 (Winter 2001): 16.

131. Dana 465.

132. Turner 40-2.

133. Turner 39-40.

134. Mouin Rabbani. "Palestinian, Israeli Rule." *The Struggle for Sovereignty* Eds. Joel Beinin and Rebecca L. Stein. (Stanford, CA: Stanford UP, 2006). 76-7.

135. Rabbani "Palestinian, Israeli Rule" 79.

136. Hammami and Tamari 6.

137. Turner 41.

138. Turner 42.

139. Rabbani "Palestinian, Israeli Rule" 81.

140. Seitz 123.

141. Dana 465.

142. Charlotte Kates, "Palestinian Security Cooperation and the Internationalization of Occupation: The Case of Ahmad Sa'adat," *Jadaliyya*, 27 January 2015, <http://cities.jadaliyya.com/pages/index/20665/palestinian-authority-security-cooperation-and-the>.

143. Kates.

144. Turner 42.

145. Kates.

146. Dana 463.

147. Dana 463.

148. Rabbani "Palestinian, Israeli Rule" 80-1.

149. Turner 44.

150. Dana 469-73.

151. Dana 469-73.

152. Dana 469-73.

153. Dana 474.

154. Turner 43.

155. Adam Hanieh, "Palestine in the Middle East: Opposing Neoliberalism and US Power Part 1," *MRonline*, 19 July 2008. <http://mrzine.monthlyreview.org/2008/hanieh190708a.html>.

156. Turner 45.

157. Turner 37-8.

158. Hammami and Tamari 17-18.

159. Hammami and Tamari 17.

160. Joel Beinin. "The Oslo Process and the Limits of a Pax Americana." 34.

CHAPTER THREE: ISRAEL DOES NOT HAVE A RIGHT TO DEFEND ITSELF

1. "Israeli-Palestinian Collision Course," editorial, *The New York Times* 7 June 2014.

2. "Israel's War in Gaza," editorial, *The New York Times* 19 July 2014.

3. United Nations Human Rights Council, *Report of the Detailed Findings of the Independent Commission of Inquiry Established Pursuant to Human Rights Council Resolution S-21/1*, A/HRC/29/52 (22 June 2015), available from <http://www.ohchr.org/EN/HRBodies/HRC/CoIGazaConflict/Pages/ReportCoIGaza.aspx#report>. 31.

4. Nicolas Pelham. "Gaza's Tunnel Phenomenon: The Unintended Dynamics of Israel's Siege." *Journal of Palestine Studies* XL1.4 (Summer 2012): 6-8.

5. Pelham 16.

6. Pelham 16.

7. Seitz 124.

8. Seitz 124.

9. Seitz 124-5.

10. Nancy Kanwisher, Johannes Haushofer, & Anat Biletzki, "Reigniting Violence: How Do Ceasefires End?" *Huffington Post*, <http://www.huffingtonpost.com/nancy-kanwisher/reigniting-violence-how-d_b_155611.html>.

11. Nancy Kanwisher, Johannes Haushofer, & Anat Biletzki.

12. "Wanted Militant Dies in Gaza Raid," *BBC*, 8 June 2006, <http://news.bbc.co.uk/2/hi/middle_east/5062360.stm>.

13. Sean Alfano, "Hamas Wants Out of Truce With Israel," *CBS*, 9 June 2006. <http://www.cbsnews.com/news/hamas-wants-out-of-truce-with-israel/>.

14. "11 Palestinians, Including a Man, His Two Children and Two paramedics, Killed and 30 Others Wounded in an IOF Air Strike on a Civilian Car in Gaza," *Palestine Centre for Human Rights*, 13 June 2006. <http://pchrgaza.org/en/?p=2984>.

15. Ian Fisher, "2 Palestinian Children Die in Israeli Strike on Gaza," *The New York Times*, 20 June 2006. <http://www.nytimes.com/2006/06/20/world/middleeast/20cnd-israel.html>.

16. "Israel Captures Pair in Gaza Raid," *BBC*, 24 June 2006, <http://news.bbc.co.uk/2/hi/middle_east/5112846.stm>.

17. Steven Erlanger, "Tensions Rise After Israeli is Kidnapped," *The New York Times*, 26 June 2006, <http://www.nytimes.com/2006/06/26/world/middleeast/26cnd-mideast.html>.

18. Berrigan 17.

19. Michele K. Esposito, "Prelude to Operation Cast Lead: Israel's Unilerateral Disengagement to the Eve of War," *Journal of Palestine Studies* 38.3 (Spring 2009): 167.

20. Esposito 167.

21. Mouin Rabbani, "Bibi's First War," *London Review of Books*, 17 November 2012, <http://www.lrb.co.uk/blog/2012/11/17/mouin-rabbani/bibis-first-war/>.

22. Rabbani "Bibi's First War."

23. Reuven Pedatzur. "Why Did Isael Kill Jabari?" *Haaretz*, 04 December 2012, <http://www.haaretz.com/opinion/why-did-israel-kill-jabari. premium-1.482224>.

24. Aluf Benn, "Israel Killed Its Subcontractor in Gaza," *Haaretz*, 14 November 2012, <http://www.haaretz.com/israel-news/isra-el-killed-its-subcontractor-in-gaza.premium-1.477886>.

25. Pedatzur.

26. Nathan Thrall. "How the West Chose War in Gaza." *New York Times* 17 July 2014: A23.

27. Peter Beaumont. "Palestinian Unity Government of Fatah and Hamas Sworn In." *The Guardian*, 2 June 2014 <https://www.theguardian.com/world/2014/jun/02/palestinian-unity-government-sworn-in-fatah-hamas>

28. Thrall A23.

29. "Ceasefire Violations," *Visualizing Palestine*, 2 July 2014, <http://visualizingpalestine.org/visuals/gaza-ceasefire-violations>.

30. Benny Morris, "The Israeli Press and the Qibya Operation." *Journal of Palestine Studies* 25.4 (Summer 1996): 41.

31. Noam Chomsky, "International Terrorism: Image and Reality." *Crime and Social Justice* 27/28 (1987): 186.

32. Chomsky "International Terrorism" 186.

33. Morris 41.

34. Morris 41.

35. Morris 41.

36. Shira Robinson, "Local Struggle, National Struggle: Palestinian Responses to the Kafr Qasim Massacre and its Aftermath, 1956-1966." *International Journal of Middle East Studies* 35 (2003): 393.

37. Nur Masalha, "The 1956-57 Occupation of the Gaza Strip: Israeli Proposals to Resettle the Palestinian Refugees." *British Journal of Middle Eastern Studies* 23. 1 (May 1996): 59.

38. Nur Masalha "The 1956-57 Occupation of the Gaza Strip" 60.

39. Rashid Khalidi *Sowing Crisis* 147.

40. Pappe *A History of Modern Palestine* 223.

41. "Fatalities in the First Intifada," *B'Tselem*, <http://www.btselem.org/statistics/first_intifada_tables>.

42. "Fatalities in the First Intifada," *B'Tselem*.

43. "Intifada Toll 2000-2005," *BBC*, 8 February 2005, <http://news.bbc.co.uk/2/hi/middle_east/3694350.stm>.

44. "Intifada Toll 2000-2005," *BBC*.

45. "Broken Lives—A Year of Intifada," *Amnesty International*, 13 November 2001, <https://www.amnesty.org/en/documents/MDE15/083/2001/en/>.

46. August Richard Norton. *Hezbollah: A Short History*. (Princeton, NJ: Princeton UP, 2007.) 84.

47. "Israel/Lebanon: Unlawful Killings During Operation Grapes of Wrath," *Amnesty International*, 23 July 1996. <https://www.amnesty.org/en/documents/MDE15/042/1996/en/>.

48. Norton 84.

49. Norton 87.

50. Khalidi *Sowing Crisis* 215.

51. Amnesty International, *Amnesty International Report 2007 - Lebanon*, 23 May 2007, available at <http://www.refworld.org/docid/46558ed37.htm>.

52. Amnesty International, *Amnesty International Report 2007 – Lebanon*.

53. "Wanted Militant Dies in Gaza Raid," *BBC*.

54. Bergman.

55. United Nations, General Assembly, "Special Committee Calls for Security Council Sanctions Against Israel for 'Culture of Impunity'

Regarding Arab Rights in Occupied Lands," GA/SPD/361 (6 November 2006), available from <http://www.un.org/press/en/2006/gaspd361.doc.htm>.

56. "A Special Report on Israel's Restrictions of Palestinian Right of Movement at Rafah Crossing," *Al-Mezan Centre for Human Rights*, February 2007, <http://www.mezan.org/en/post/2567/A+SPECIAL+REPORT+ON+ISRAEL%E2%80%99S+RESTRICTIONS+OF+PALESTINIAN+RIGHT+OF+MOVE-MENT+AT+RAFAH+CROSSING%3Cbr%3EGAZA,+February+2007>. 7.

57. "A Special Report on Israel's Restrictions of Palestinian Right of Movement at Rafah Crossing," *Al-Mezan Centre for Human Rights* 14.

58. "Israeli Military Actions Criticized at First UN Human Rights Council Special Session," *UN News Centre*, 5 July 2006. <http://www.un.org/apps/news/story.asp?NewsID=19108&#.V9_zKK3qsq4>.

59. "Israeli Military Actions Criticized at First UN Human Rights Council Special Session," *UN News Centre.*

60. "Israeli Military Actions Criticized at First UN Human Rights Council Special Session," *UN News Centre.*

61. Esposito 166-7.

62. "Rain of Fire," *Human Rights Watch*, 25 March 2009, <https://www.hrw.org/report/2009/03/25/rain-fire/israels-unlaw-ful-use-white-phosphorus-gaza>.

63. "Israel/Gaza: Operation "Cast Lead": 22 Days of Death and Destruction," *Amnesty International*, 2 July 2009, < https://www.amnesty.org/en/documents/MDE15/015/2009/en/>. 1.

64. "Fatalities During Cast Lead," *B'Tselem*, <http://www.btselem.org/statistics/fatalities/during-cast-lead/by-date-of-event>.

65. "Fatalities During Cast Lead," *B'Tselem.*

66. Adam Shatz, "Why Israel Didn't Win," *London Review of Books*, 6 December 2012, <http://www.lrb.co.uk/v34/n23/adam-shatz/why-israel-

didnt-win>.

67. "Through Women's Eyes: A PCHR Report on the Gender-Specific Impact and Consequences of Operation Cast Lead," *Palestine Centre for Human Rights*, 28 September 2009, <https://pchrgaza.org/en/?p=4738>.

68. "Israel: Gaza Airstrikes Violated Laws of War," *Human Rights Watch*, 12 February 2013, <https://www.hrw.org/news/2013/02/12/israel-gaza-airstrikes-violated-laws-war>.

69. United Nations Human Rights Council, *Report of the United Nations High Commissioner for Human Rights on the implementation of Human Rights Council resolutions S-9/1 and S-12/*, A/HRC/22/35 (6 March 2013), available from <http://www.ohchr.org/Documents/HRBodies/HRCouncil/RegularSession/Session22/A.HRC.22.35_AUV.pdf>. 4.

70. Avi Shlaim. "The Iron Wall Revisited." 80.

71. Avi Shlaim. "The Iron Wall Revisited." 81.

72. Darryl Li. "The Gaza Strip As Laboratory: Notes in the Wake of Disengagement." *Journal of Palestine Studies* 35.2 (Winter 2006): 39.

73. Joseph Massad. *The Persistence of the Palestinian Question: Essays on Zionism and the Palestinians*. Oxon, UK: Routledge, 2006. 143.

74. Massad 152.

75. Steven Salaita, "Liberal Zionism and the Ethnonational Imperative," *Electronic Intifada*, 30 December 2015, <https://electronicintifada.net/blogs/steven-salaita/liberal-zionism-and-ethnonational-imperative>.

76. Sara Roy. "Reconceptualizing the Israeli-Palestinian Conflict: Key Paradigm Shifts." *Journal of Palestine Studies* XL1.3 (Spring 2012): 73.

77. Sara Roy. "Reconceptualizing the Israeli-Palestinian Conflict." 73.

78. Sara Roy. "Reconceptualizing the Israeli-Palestinian Conflict." 73.

79. Tamari.

80. Tamari.

81. Francesco Chiodelli. "The Jerusalem Master Plan: Planning Into the Conflict." *Jerusalem Quarterly* 51: 13.

82. Andrew Clarno. *The Empire's New Walls: Sovereignty, Neo-liberalism, and the Production of Space in Post-apartheid South Africa and Post-Oslo Palestine/Israel*. Unpublished Dissertation. 205

83. Clarno 214.

84. Francesco Chiodelli. "The Jerusalem Master Plan." *Jerusalem Quarterly* 51: 13.

85. Clarno 210.

86. Sara Roy. "Reconceptualizing the Israeli-Palestinian Conflict." 73-4.

87. Darryl Li. "The Gaza Strip As Laboratory: Notes in the Wake of Disengagement." *Journal of Palestine Studies* 35.2 (Winter 2006): 45.

88. Li 45.

89. Sara Roy. "Economic Siege and Political Isolation: The Gaza Strip in the Second Intifada." *The Struggle for Sovereignty* Eds. Joel Beinin and Rebecca L. Stein. (Stanford, CA: Stanford UP, 2006). 283.

90. Roy "Economic Siege and Political Isolation" 286.

91. Jonathan Cook, "Israel's Starvation Diet for Gaza," *Electronic Intifada*, 24 October 2012, <https://electronicintifada.net/content/israels-starvation-diet-gaza/11810>.

92. Cook, "Israel's Starvation Diet for Gaza."

93. Cook, "Israel's Starvation Diet for Gaza."

94. "Gaza Under Pressure: Gaza Needs Much Improved Access to Essential Supplies," *ICRCblog*, 13 April 2014. <http://blogs.icrc.org/ilot/2014/04/13/gaza-under-pressure-gazans-require-much-improved-access-to-essential-supplies/>.

CONCLUSION

1. Joseph Uscinski. *The People's News*. New York: NYU P, 2014. 4.

2. Lawrence Solely and Robert L. Craig, "Advertising Pressures on

Newspapers: A Survey." *Journal of Advertising* 21.4 (December 1992): 1.

3. Soontae An and Lori Bergen. "Advertiser Pressure on Daily Newspapers." *Journal of Advertising* 36.2 (Summer 2007): 118.

4. An and Bergen 111.

5. Uscinski 9.

6. Hirji 394.

7. Uscinski 13.

8. Entman 57.

9. Hirji 394.

10. Seth Ashley. "The Sociology of Media System Structure." *Javnost-The Public* 21.3 (2014): 18.

11. Entman 55.

WORKS CITED

"11 Palestinians, Including a Man, His Two Children and Two paramedics, Killed and 30 Others Wounded in an IOF Air Strike on a Civilian Car in Gaza," *Palestine Centre for Human Rights*, 13 June 2006. <http://pchrgaza.org/en/?p=2984>.

"20 Facts: 20 Years Since the Oslo Accords," *Oxfam*, 13 September 2013, available at <https://www.oxfam.org/en/pressroom/pressreleases/2013-09-13/20-years-missed-opportunity-has-undermined-progress-israel>. Accessed 18 August 2016.

"50 Days: More Than 500 Children," *B'Tselem*, <http://www.btselem.org/2014_gaza_conflict/en/il/>. Accessed 13 September 2016.

Abdo, Nahla. "Women, War, and Peace: Reflection From the Intifada." *Women's Studies International Forum* 25.5 (2002): 585-93.

Abukhalil, As'ad. "The Left and The Syria Debate." *Jadaliyya*. 10 December 2016, <http://www.jadaliyya.com/pages/index/25628/the-left-and-the-syria-debate>. Accessed 20 April 2017.

Abdulhadi, Raba. "Imagining Justice and Peace in the Age of Empire." *Peace Review* 16.1 (March 2004): 85-9.

Abu-Lughod, Ibrahim. "Territorially-Based Nationalism and the Politics of Negation." *Blaming the Victims* Ed. Edward Said and Christopher Hitchens. London: Verso, 1988. 193-206.

Abu-Manneh, Bashir. "Israel in the U.S Empire." *Monthly Review* 58.10 (March 2007), <http://monthlyreview.org/2007/03/01/israel-in-the-u-s-empire/>. Accessed 9 February 2017.

Abunimah, Ali. "Obama "Peace" Envoy Ridicules Notion That Palestinians Have "Rights."" *Electronic Intifada*, 9 May 2014 <https://electronicintifada.net/blogs/ali-abunimah/obama-peace-envoy-ridicules-notion-palestinians-have-rights>. Accessed 30 March 2017.

—. "What's Behind Hamas' New Charter?" Electronic Intifdada, 2 May 2017. https://electronicintifada.net/blogs/ali-abunimah/whats-behind-hamas-new-charter>. Accessed 2 May 2017.

"Administrative Detention." *B'Tselem*, 21 September 2014. <http://www.btselem.org/administrative_detention>.

Advisory Opinion Concerning Legal Consequences of the Construction of a Wall in the Occupied Palestinian Territory, International Court of Justice (ICJ), 9 July 2004, available at <http://www.icj-cij.org/docket/index.php?pr=71&code=mwp&p1=3&p2=4&p3=6>. Accessed 21 September 2016.

Ajl, Max. "The Biggest Israel Aid Deal in History Will Bolster Occupation and the U.S. Defense Industry." *In These Times.* 20 September 2016. <http://inthesetimes.com/article/19479/the-israeli-aid-package-10-more-years-of-the-special-relationship>. Accessed 21 September 2016.

Akram, Fares. "Israel Threatens to Step Up Gaza Campaign." *Al-Jazeera.* 16 July 2014. <http://www.aljazeera.com/news/middleeast/2014/07/israeli-strikes-resume-after-brief-gaza-calm-201471511044177114.html>. Accessed 18 August 2016.

Alfano, Sean. "Hamas Wants Out of Truce With Israel." *CBS*, 9 June 2006. <http://www.cbsnews.com/news/hamas-wants-out-of-truce-with-israel/>. Accessed 18 October 2016.

Amnesty International, *Amnesty International Report 2007 - Lebanon* , 23 May 2007, available at <http://www.refworld.org/docid/46558ed37. htm>. Accessed 14 March 2017.

An, Soontae and Lori Bergen. "Advertiser Pressure on Daily Newspapers." *Journal of Advertising* 36.2 (Summer 2007): 111-21.

"Another Bloody Day of the Israeli Offensive on Gaza: Dozens Palestinian Civilians Killed or Wounded by Israeli Attacks in Khuza'a, 'Abassan and al-Qarara Villages; Israeli Forces Attack Gaza from the Air, the Sea and the Ground; More Palestinians Forcibly," *Palestine Centre for Human Rights*, 24 July 2014, <http://pchrgaza.org/ en/?p=1612>. Accessed 1 June 2016.

"Annual Report: Israel and the Occupied Palestinian Territories 2013," *Amnesty International*, 23 May 2013, <http://www.amnestyusa. org/research/reports/annual-report-israel-and-the-occupied-palestinian-territories-2013?page=show>. Accessed 2 August 2016.

"Anti-Boycott Law," *Adalah*, <https://www.adalah.org/en/law/view/492>. Accessed 9 August 2016.

"Arab Minority Rights," *The Association for Civil Rights in Israel*, <http://www.acri.org.il/en/category/arab-citizens-of-israel/arab-minority-rights/>. Accessed 16 August 2016.

Ashley, Seth. "The Sociology of Media System Structure." *Javnost-The Public* 21.3 (2014): 5-21.

"BADIL is proud to announce the release of its biennial Survey of Palestinian Refugees and Internally Displaced Persons 2010–2012," *BADIL*, <http://www.badil.org/en/press-releases/142-2012/3638-press-eng-53?pid=20>. Accessed 28 July 2016.

"Ban on Family Unification," *Adalah*, <https://www.adalah.org/en/law/ view/511>. Accessed 9 August 2016.

Baskin, Gershon. "What Israel Must Do Now," *Slate*, 10 August 2014. <http://www.slate.com/articles/news_and_politics/foreigners/2014/08/gaza_war_continues_here_s_what_israel_needs_to_do_to_hurt_hamas_and_help.html>. Accessed 17 August 2016.

Beaumont, Peter. "Palestinian Unity Government of Fatah and Hamas Sworn In." *The Guardian*, 2 June 2014, www.theguardian.com/world/2014/jun/02/palestinian-unity-government-sworn-in-fatah-hamas. Accessed 6 June 2016.

Beinin, Joel. "Confronting Settlement Expansion in East Jerusalem." *Middle East Research and Information Project*, 14 February 2010, <http://www.merip.org/mero/mero021410>. Accessed 8 March 2017.

—. "The Oslo Process and the Limits of a Pax Americana." *The Struggle for Sovereignty* Eds. Joel Beinin and Rebecca L. Stein. (Stanford, CA: Stanford UP, 2006): 21-37.

Benn, Aluf. "Israel Killed Its Subcontractor in Gaza." *Haaretz*, 14 November 2012. <http://www.haaretz.com/israel-news/israel-killed-its-subcontractor-in-gaza.premium-1.477886>. Accessed 2 March 2017.

Bergman, Ronen. "Gilad Shalit and the Rising Price of an Israeli Life." *The New York Times*, 13 November 2011, <http://www.nytimes.com/2011/11/13/magazine/gilad-shalit-and-the-cost-of-an-israeli-life.html?pagewanted=all>. Accessed 31 January 2017.

Berrigan, Frida. "Made in the U.S.A: American Military Aid to Israel." *Journal of Palestine Studies* 38.3 (Spring 2009): 6-21.

Bloodworth, James. "The Middle East Debate Has More to Do With the Fashion for Revolutionary Tourism Than Real Politics," *The Independent*, 14 July 2014. <http://www.independent.co.uk/voices/

comment/arguments-about-israel-and-palestine-have-more-to-do-with-the-fashion-for-revolutionary-tourism-than-9604934.html>. Accessed 13 July 2016.

"Broken Lives—A Year of Intifada," *Amnesty International*, 13 November 2001, <https://www.amnesty.org/en/documents/MDE15/083/2001/en/>. Accessed 8 February 2017.

Cappella, Joseph N. and Kathleen Hall Jamieson. *Spiral of Cynicism*. NY: Oxford UP, 1997.

"A Ceasefire for Gaza," editorial, *The Washington Post*, 30 July 2014.

"Ceasefire Violations," *Visualizing Palestine*, 2 July 2014, <http://visualizingpalestine.org/visuals/gaza-ceasefire-violations>. Accessed 9 March 2017.

Chiodelli, Francesco. "The Jerusalem Master Plan: Planning Into the Conflict." *Jerusalem Quarterly* 51: 5-20.

Chomsky, Noam. *The Fateful Triangle*. Montreal: Black Rose, 1984.

—. "International Terrorism: Image and Reality." *Crime and Social Justice* 27/28 (1987): 172-200.

Clarno, Andrew. *The Empire's New Walls: Sovereignty, Neo-liberalism, and the Production of Space in Post-apartheid South Africa and Post-Oslo Palestine/Israel*. Unpublished Dissertation.

Cohen, Michael. "Is the Arab-Israeli Conflict Going to be the War That Never Ends?" *The Observer* 3 August 2014: OB 32.

Cohen, Nick. "Homophobia is Now Met With the Same Silence Given to Homophobia." *The Spectator* 13 June 2016. <http://blogs.spectator.co.uk/2016/06/homophobic-murder-will-gays-become-new-jews/>. Accessed 29 June 2016.

Cook, Jonathan. "Israel's Starvation Diet for Gaza," *Electronic Intifada*, 24 October 2012, <https://electronicintifada.net/content/israels-starvation-diet-gaza/11810>. 28 March 2017.

—. "Peace Process is Doomed to Fail While Israel Stalls for Time," *The National*, 29 October 2013, <http://www.thenational.ae/thenationalconversation/comment/peace-process-is-doomed-to-fail-while-israel-stalls-for-time#full>. Accessed 30 March 2017.

Cronin, David. "Warren Buffett Signs $2 Billion Check in Support of Israeli Apartheid." *Electronic Intifada*, 6 May 2013. <https://electronicintifada.net/blogs/david-cronin/warren-buffett-signs-2-billion-check-support-israeli-apartheid>. 28 March 2017.

Dana, Tariq. "The Symbiosis Between Palestinian 'Fayyadism' and Israeli 'Economic Peace': The Political Economy of Capitalist Peace in the Context of Colonisation." *Conflict, Security & Development* 15.5 (December 2015): 455-77.

"Discriminatory Water Supply," *B'Tselem*, 27 September 2016. <http://www.btselem.org/water/discrimination_in_water_supply>. Accessed 16 August 2016.

Entman, Robert. "Framing: Toward a Clarification of a Fractured Paradigm." *Journal of Communication* 43.4 (Autumn 1993): 51-8.

Erakat, Noura, Rashid Khalidi, and Mouin Rabbani. "FAQ on Failed Effort to Arrange a Ceasefire Between Israel and Hamas." *Jadaliyya* 16 July 2014. <http://www.jadaliyya.com/pages/index/18577/faq-on-failed-effort-to-arrange-ceasefire-between-> Accessed 13 June 2016.

Erlanger, Steven. "Tensions Rise After Israeli is Kidnapped," *The New York Times*, 26 June 2006, <http://www.nytimes.com/2006/06/26/world/middleeast/26cnd-mideast.html>. 18 October 2016.

Esposito, Michelle K. "Prelude to Operation Cast Lead: Israel's Unilererateral Disengagement to the Eve of War." *Journal of Palestine Studies* 38.3 (Spring 2009): 139-168.

"Fatalities During Cast Lead," *B'Tselem*, <http://www.btselem.org/statistics/fatalities/during-cast-lead/by-date-of-event>. Accessed 1 February 2017.

"Fatalities in the First Intifada," *B'Tselem*, <http://www.btselem.org/statistics/first_intifada_tables>.

Fisher, Ian. "2 Palestinian Children Die in Israeli Strike on Gaza," *The New York Times*, 20 June 2006. <http://www.nytimes.com/2006/06/20/world/middleeast/20cnd-israel.html>. Accessed 20 October 2016.

"Four Horrific Killings," editorial, *The New York Times* 8 July 2014.

Freedland, Jonathan. "This Endless Point-Scoring Brings Us No Closer to Peace: Those Who Support Israel or Palestine as if They Were Rival Football Teams Do Those Two Peoples a Terrible Disservice." *The Guardian* 24 November 2012: GRDN 55.

—. "Israel's Fears are Real but This War is Utterly Self-Defeating." *The Guardian* 26 July 2014: GRDN 41.

—. "This Cycle of Vengeance Could Start a Third Intifada," *The Guardian*, 5 July 14: GRDN 33.

"Gaza: Two Years Since The 2014 Hostilities." *United Nations Office for the Coordination of Humanitarian Affairs*. 30 August 2016. < https://www.ochaopt.org/content/gaza-two-years-2014-hostilities-august-2016> Accessed 13 September 2016.

"Gaza: Israel Must Stop Bombing Civilians," *Doctors Without Borders*, 20 July 2014, <http://www.doctorswithoutborders.org/news-stories/

press-release/gaza-israel-must-stop-bombing-trapped-civilians>. Accessed 5 July 2016.

"Gaza's Mounting Death Toll," editorial, *The New York Times* 25 July 2014.

"Gaza Under Pressure: Gaza Needs Much Improved Access to Essential Supplies," *ICRCblog*, 13 April 2014. <http://blogs.icrc.org/ilot/2014/04/13/gaza-under-pressure-gazans-require-much-improved-access-to-essential-supplies/>. 22 March 2017.

Goldberg, Jeffrey. "The Paranoid, Supremacist Roots of the Stabbing Intifada," *The Atlantic*, 16 Oct 2015. <https://www.theatlantic.com/international/archive/2015/10/the-roots-of-the-palestinian-uprising-against-israel/410944/>. Accessed 13 September 2016.

Goodman, HA. "It's Immoral for Hamas to Use Human Shields and Immoral for Israel to Bomb Human Shields," *Huffington Post*, <http://www.huffingtonpost.com/h-a-goodman/its-immoral-for-hamas-to_b_5629548.html>. Accessed 20 July 2016.

Gore, Will. "When Both Palestinians and Israelis Think We are Biased, We Must Be Doing Something Right," *The Independent*, 13 July 2014. <http://www.independent.co.uk/voices/comment/when-both-palestinians-and-israelis-think-we-are-biased-we-must-be-doing-something-right-9603068.html>. Accessed 20 July 2016.

Guarnieri, Mya. "What Does Israeli 'Acceptance' of Ceasefire Really Mean?" *+972 Magazine*, 15 July 2014, <https://972mag.com/what-does-israeli-acceptance-of-ceasefire-really-mean/93642/>. Accessed 10 August 2016.

Hajjar, Lisa. "Is Gaza Occupied and Why Does it Matter?" *Jadaliyya*, 14 July 2014, <http://www.jadaliyya.com/pages/index/8807/is-gaza-still-occupied-and-why-does-it-matter>. Accessed 8 July 2016.

Hammami, Rema and Salim Tamari. "The Second Uprising: End or New Beginning?" *Journal of Palestine Studies* 30.2 (Winter 2001): 5-25.

Hanieh, Adam. "From State-Led Growth to Globalization: the Evolution of Israeli Capitalism," *Journal of Palestine Studies* 32.4 (Summer 2003): 14. "From State-Led Growth to Globalization: the Evolution of Israeli Capitalism," *Journal of Palestine Studies* 32.4 (Summer 2003): 5-

—. Palestine in the Middle East: Opposing Neoliberalism and US Power Part 1," *MRonline*, 19 July 2008. <http://mrzine.monthlyreview.org/2008/hanieh190708a.html>. Accessed 13 January 2017.

—. "Palestine in the Middle East: Opposing Neoliberalism and US Power Part 2," *MRonline*, 19 July 2008 <http://mrzine.monthlyreview.org/2008/hanieh190708b.html>. Accessed 13 January 2017.

Harris. "Why Don't I Criticize Israel?" *SamHarris.org*, 27 July 2014. <https://www.samharris.org/podcast/item/why-dont-i-criticize-israel>. Accessed 13 September 2016.

Hersh, Seymour. "The Redirection." *The New Yorker*. 5 March 2007. <http://www.newyorker.com/magazine/2007/03/05/the-redirection>. Accessed 20 April 2017.

Higgins, Andrew. "How Israel Helped to Spawn Hamas." *Wall Street Journal*, Eastern Edition 24 January 2009: W1.

Hirji, Faiza. "The Colour of Difference: Race, Diversity, and Journalism in Canada." *Mediascapes: New Patterns in Canadian Communication*. Ed. Leslie Regan Shade. Fourth Edition. Toronto: Nelson, 2014. 290-408.

"HP Labs Israel Celebrates 20 Years of Innovation," *Hewlett Packard Enterprise Community*, 22 May 2014 <https://community.hpe.

com/t5/Behind-the-scenes-Labs/HP-Labs-Israel-celebrates-20-years-of-innovation/ba-p/6793252#.WNrRK6K1vIU>. Accessed 28 March 2017.

Hroub, Khaled. *Hamas: A Beginner's Guide*. 2nd ed. Ann Arbor, Mich: Pluto, 2010.

"In Figures," *United Nations Relief and Works Agency*, January 2014, <https://www.unrwa.org/sites/default/files/2014_01_uif_-_english.pdf>.

"Intifada Toll 2000-2005," *BBC*, 8 February 2005, <http://news.bbc.co.uk/2/hi/middle_east/3694350.stm>. Accessed 15 March 2017.

"Israel Captures Pair in Gaza Raid," *BBC*, 24 June 2006, <http://news.bbc.co.uk/2/hi/middle_east/5112846.stm>. Accessed 20 October 2016.

"Israel-Hamas Peace Agreement Text," *Huffington Post*, 21 November 2012. <http://www.huffingtonpost.com/2012/11/21/israel-hamas-peace-agreement-text_n_2171602.html>. Access 29 June 2016.

"Israel, Hamas and the Rockets; The Level of Civilian Deaths in Gaza is unacceptable," editorial, *Financial Times*, 23 July 2014: FTFT USA Ed 1 06.

"Israel: Gaza Airstrikes Violated Laws of War," *Human Rights Watch*, 12 February 2013, <https://www.hrw.org/news/2013/02/12/israel-gaza-airstrikes-violated-laws-war>. Accessed 8 July 2015.

Israel/Gaza Conflict: Questions and Answers," Amnesty International, 25 July 2014, <https://www.amnesty.org/en/latest/news/2014/07/israelgaza-conflict-questions-and-answers/>. Accessed 15 February 2017.

"Israel/Gaza: Attacks on Medical Facilities and Civilians Add to War Crime Allegations," *Amnesty International*, 21 July 2014, <https://

www.amnesty.org/en/latest/news/2014/07/israelgaza-attacks-medical-facilities-and-civilians-add-war-crime-allegations/>. Accessed 22 June 2016.

"Israel/Gaza: Operation "Cast Lead": 22 Days of Death and Destruction," *Amnesty International,* 2 July 2009, <https://www.amnesty.org/en/documents/MDE15/015/2009/en/>. 1. Accessed 13 February 2017.

"Israeli Forces Shoot and Kill Two Palestinian Teens Near Ramallah," *Defense for Children International,* 17 May 2014, <www.dci-palestine.org/israeli_forces_shoot_and_kill_two_palestinian_teens_near_ramallah. Accesed 20 June 2016>. Accessed 8 July 2016.

"Israeli Military Actions Criticized at First UN Human Rights Council Special Session," *UN News Centre,* 5 July 2006. <http://www.un.org/apps/news/story.asp?NewsID=19108&#.V9_zKK3qsq4>. Accessed 7 February 2017.

"Israeli-Palestinian Collision Course," editorial, *The New York Times* 7 June 2014.

"Israel/Lebanon: Unlawful Killings During Operation Grapes of Wrath," *Amnesty International,* 23 July 1996. <https://www.amnesty.org/en/documents/MDE15/042/1996/en/>. Accessed 14 February 2017.

"Israel-Palestine—Glimmers of Sanity Amid the Tragic Killings." Editorial. *The Observer* 6 July 2014: OB 32.

"Israel's Worldwide Role in Repression," *International Jewish Anti-Zionist Network,* 2012, <https://israelglobalrepression.files.wordpress.com/2012/12/israels-worldwide-role-in-repression-footnotes-finalized.pdf >. Accessed 20 April 2017.

"Israel Says Separation Wall Will Be Border," *Al-Jazeera,* 5 November 2013, <http://www.aljazeera.com/news/middleeast/2013/11/

israel-says-separation-wall-will-be-border-201311514132609960.
html>. Accessed 30 March 2017.

"Israel's War in Gaza," editorial, *The New York Times* 19 July 2014.

"Jewish National Fund Law," *Adalah*, <https://www.adalah.org/en/law/
view/531>. Accessed 9 August 2016.

Jewish Telegraphic Agency, "US Billionaire Warren Buffet Invests $5M in
Israel Bonds, Helps Raise $60M." *Times of Israel*, 8 November 2016.
<http://www.timesofisrael.com/us-billionaire-warren-buffett-invests-
5m-in-israel-bonds-helps-raise-60m/>. Accessed 28 March 2017.

"Joint input to the ENP Country Report on Israel 2013 Human rights
of prisoners and detainees held in Israel, with focus on Torture /
CIDT1." *Adalah, Al Mezan Centre for Human Rights, Physicians
for Human Rights-Israel, Public Committee Against Torture in
Israel,* October 2013, <https://www.adalah.org/uploads/oldfiles/
Public/files/English/International_Advocacy/ENP/Joint-input-
Prisoners-ENP-Israel-Oct-2013.pdf>. Accessed 22 March 2017.

Kelly, Matthew. "US Middle East Policy and the State-Capital Controversy
in Imperialism's Historiography." *Middle East Critique* 23.1 (2014):
73-88.

Kanwisher, Nancy, Johannes Haushofer, & Anat Biletzki. "Reigniting
Violence: How Do Ceasefires End?" *Huffington Post*, <http://www.
huffingtonpost.com/nancy-kanwisher/reigniting-violence-how-
d_b_155611.html>. Accessed 12 October 2016.

Kates, Charlotte. "Palestinian Authority Security Cooperation and the
Internationalization of Occupation: The Case of Ahmad Sa'adat,"
Jadaliyya, 27 January 2015, <http://cities.jadaliyya.com/pages/
index/20665/palestinian-authority-security-cooperation-and-
the>. Accessed 30 March 2017.

Khalidi, Rashid. *Brokers of Deceit*. Boston: Beacon, 2013.

—. *The Iron Cage*. Boston: Beacon, 2006.

—. *Sowing Crisis*. Boston: Beacon, 2009.

Khalili, Laleh. "The Location of Palestine in Global Counterinsurgencies." *International Journal of Middle East Studies* 42.3 (August 2010):

Kohn, Sally. "Why I'm Against Hamas, Against What Israel Is Doing, and For Judaism," *Daily Beast*, 25 July 2014. <http://www.thedailybeast.com/articles/2014/07/25/why-i-m-against-hamas-against-what-israel-is-doing-and-for-judaism.html>. Accessed 8 July 2016.

Lewis, Ori. "Israel Announces Plans for Building 1,400 Settlement Homes," *Reuters*, 10 January 2014, <http://www.reuters.com/article/us-palestinians-israel-settlements-idUSBREA090KW20140110>. Accessed 30 March 2017.

Li, Darryl. "The Gaza Strip As Laboratory: Notes in the Wake of Disengagement." *Journal of Palestine Studies* 35.2 (Winter 2006): 38-55.

"Making the Gaza Cease-Fire Last," editorial, *The New York Times* 7 August 2014.

Masalha, Nur. Nur Masalha, "The 1956-57 Occupation of the Gaza Strip: Israeli Proposals to Resettle the Palestinian Refugees." *British Journal of Middle Eastern Studies* 23. 1 (May 1996): 59.

—. "The Palestinian Nakba: Zionism, 'Transfer' and the 1948 Exodus." *Global Dialogue* 4.3 (Summer 2002): 77-91. 84.

Morris, Benny. "The Israeli Press and the Qibya Operation." *Journal of Palestine Studies* 25.4 (Summer 1996): 40-52.

Massad, Joseph. *The Persistence of the Palestinian Question: Essays on Zionism and the Palestinians*. Oxon, UK: Routledge, 2006. 152.

"Nakba Law," *Adalah*, <https://www.adalah.org/en/law/view/496>. Accessed 9 August 2016.

Nelson, Sara C. "Unarmed Palestinian Teens 'Shot Dead By Israeli Troops': UN Demands Investigation." *Huffington Post*, 21 May 2014, www.huffingtonpost.co.uk/2014/05/21/unarmed-palestinian-teens-shot-dead-israeli-troops-un-demands-investigation_n_5363300.html. Accessed 2 June 2016.

Nitzan, Jonathan and Shimshon Bichler. *The Global Political Economy of Israel*. Lodon: Pluto, 2002.

Norton, Augustus Richard. *Hezbollah: A Short History*. Princeton, NJ: Princeton UP, 2007.

Obeidallah, Dean. "How John Stewart Made it Okay to Care About Palestinian Suffering," *Daily Beast*, 7 July 2014. <http://www.thedailybeast.com/articles/2014/07/21/how-jon-stewart-made-it-okay-to-care-about-palestinian-suffering.html>. Accessed 22 July 2016.

Occupied Palestinian Territory: Gaza Emergency Situation Report (as of 23 July 2014, 1500 hrs)" *United Nations Office for the Coordination of Humanitarian Affairs*, 23 July 2014, <https://www.ochaopt.org/content/occupied-palestinian-territory-gaza-emergency-situation-report-23-july-2014-1500-hrs>. Accessed 2 June 2016.

"Occupied Palestinian Territory: Gaza Emergency Situation Report (as of 17 July 2014, 1500 hrs)." *United Nations Office for the Coordination of Humanitarian Affairs*, 18 July 2014, www.ochaopt.org/content/occupied-palestinian-territory-gaza-emergency-situation-report-17-july-2014-1500-hrs. Accessed 1 June 2016.

"Occupied Palestinian Territory: Gaza Emergency Situation Report (as of 24 July 2014, 1500 hrs)" *United Nations Office for the Coordination of Humanitarian Affairs*, 25 July 2014, <https://www.ochaopt. org/content/occupied-palestinian-territory-gaza-emergency-situation-report-24-july-2014-1500-hrs>. Accessed 2 June 2016.

"On the 27th Day of the Israeli Offensive:Rafah Under Israeli Fire; War Crimes Committed against Palestinian Civilians; Complete Families Annihilated," *Palestine Centre for Human Rights*, 3 August 2014. <http://pchrgaza.org/en/?p=1603>. Accessed 15 July 2016.

"On the 40th anniversary of Land Day: Adalah releases new report on Israel's discriminatory land and housing policies in 2015," *Adalah*, 30 March 2016, <https://www.adalah.org/en/content/view/8771>. Accessed 15 August 2016.

Orpaz, Inbal, Amitai Ziv, and Haim Bior. "TechNation Facebook to Hire 40 for New Tel Aviv Office," *Haaretz*. 24 March 2015. <http://www.haaretz.com/israel-news/business/tech-roundup/. premium-1.648485>. Accessed 28 March 2017.

"Our Locations," *Google Careers*, <https://careers.google.com/ locations/>. Accessed 28 March 2017.

"Palestine/Israel: Indiscriminate Palestinian Rocket Attacks," *Human Rights Watch*, 9 July 2014 https://www.hrw.org/news/2014/07/09/ palestine/israel-indiscriminate-palestinian-rocket-attacks. Accessed 15 June 2016.

Pappe, Ilan. *The Ethnic Cleansing of Palestine*. London: Oneworld Publications, 2006.

—. *A History of Modern Palestine*. Cambridge: Cambridge UP, 2004.

Pedatzur, Reuven. "Why Did Isael Kill Jabari?" *Haaretz*. 04 December 2012. <http://www.haaretz.com/opinion/why-did-israel-kill-jabari.premium-1.482224>. Accessed 1 March 2017.

Peled, Yoav. "From Zionism to Capitalism," *The Struggle for Sovereignty* Eds. Joel Beinin and Rebecca L. Stein. (Stanford, CA: Stanford UP, 2006). 38-54.

Pelham, Nicolas. "Gaza's Tunnel Phenomenon: The Unintended Dynamics of Israel's Siege." *Journal of Palestine Studies* XL1.4 (Summer 2012): 6-31.

Pfeffer, Anshel. "This is Not Just a Fight Over Land, It's a Religious War." *Guardian* 21 Nov 14: GRDN 45.

Pickard, Victor. *America's Battle for Media Democracy.* New York: Cambridge UP, 2015.

"Protection of Civilians Weekly Report 10-16 June 2014," *United Nations Office for the Coordination of Humanitarian Affairs* 19 June 2014, https://www.ochaopt.org/content/protection-civilians-weekly-report-10-16-june-2014. Accessed 15 June 2016.

Rabbani, Mouin. "Bibi's First War," *London Review of Books,* 17 November 2012, <http://www.lrb.co.uk/blog/2012/11/17/mouin-rabbani/bibis-first-war/>. Accessed 26 October 2016.

—. "Palestinian Authority, Israeli Rule." *The Struggle for Sovereignty* Eds. Joel Beinin and Rebecca L. Stein. Stanford, CA: Stanford UP, 2006. 75-83.

"Rain of Fire," *Human Rights Watch,* 25 March 2009, <https://www.hrw.org/report/2009/03/25/rain-fire/israels-unlawful-use-white-phosphorus-gaza>. Accessed 8 February 2017.

Rizvi, Ali A. "7 Things to Consider Before Choosing Sides in the Middle East Conflict," Huffington Post, 28 July 2014. < http://www.huffingtonpost.com/ali-a-rizvi/picking-a-side-in-israel-palestine_b_5602701.html>. Accessed 20 July 2016.

Robinson, Shira. "Local Struggle, National Struggle: Palestinian Responses to the Kafr Qasim Massacre and its Aftermath, 1956-1966." *International Journal of Middle East Studies* 35 (2003): 393-416.

Roy, Sara. "Economic Siege and Political Isolation: The Gaza Strip in the Second Intifada." *The Struggle for Sovereignty* Eds. Joel Beinin and Rebecca L. Stein. Stanford, CA: Stanford UP, 2006. 282-87.

—. "Reconceptualizing the Israeli-Palestinian Conflict: Key Paradigm Shifts." *Journal of Palestine Studies* XL1.3 (Spring 2012): 71-91.

Said, Edward. *The Question of Palestine*. New York: Vintage, 1992.

Salaita, Steven. "Liberal Zionism and the Ethnonational Imperative," *Electronic Intifada*, 30 December 2015, <https://electronicintifada. net/blogs/steven-salaita/liberal-zionism-and-ethnonational-imperative>. Accessed 30 March 2017.

"The Scope of Israeli Control in the Gaza Strip," *B'Tselem*, 5 January 2014, http://www.btselem.org/gaza_strip/gaza_status Accessed 27 June 2016.

Seitz, Charmaine. "Coming of Age: Hamas's Rise to Prominence in the Post-Oslo Era." *The Struggle for Sovereignty* Eds. Joel Beinin and Rebecca L. Stein. Stanford, CA: Stanford UP, 2006. 112-29.

"Separate and Unequal," *Human Rights Watch*. 19 December 2010. <https://www.hrw.org/report/2010/12/19/separate-and-unequal/ israels-discriminatory-treatment-palestinians-occupied>.

"Settler Violence: Lack of Accountability," *B'Tselem*, 1 January 2011. <http://www.btselem.org/settler_violence/dual_legal_system>. Accessed 21 March 2017.

Shamah, David. "Tim Cook: Apple's Herzliya R&D Center Second-Largest in World," *Times of Israel*, 27 February 2015 <http://www.

timesofisrael.com/apples-herzliya-rd-center-now-second-largest-in-world/>. Accessed 28 March 2017.

Shatz, Adam. "Why Israel Didn't Win," *London Review of Books*, 6 December 2012, <http://www.lrb.co.uk/v34/n23/adam-shatz/why-israel-didnt-win>. Accessed 13 February 2017.

Shlaim, Avi. "The Iron Wall Revisited." *Journal of Palestine Studies* XL1.2 (Winter 2012): 80-98.

Solely, Lawrence and Robert L. Craig. "Advertising Pressures on Newspapers: A Survey." *Journal of Advertising* 21.4 (December 1992): 1-10.

"A Special Report on Israel's Restrictions of Palestinian Right of Movement at Rafah Crossing," *Al-Mezan Centre for Human Rights*, February 2007, <http://www.mezan.org/en/post/2567/A+SPECIAL+REPORT+ON+ISRAEL%E2%80%99S+RESTRIC-TIONS+OF+PALESTINIAN+RIGHT+OF+MOVEMENT+AT+RAFAH+CROSSING%3Cbr%3EGAZA,+February+2007>. 7. Accessed 22 July 2016.

"Statistics." *Addameer*, January 2017. <http://www.addameer.org/statistics/20170131>. Accessed 20 March 2017.

"Statistics." *Addameer*, May 2014. <http://www.addameer.org/statistics/20140501>. Accessed 20 March 2017.

Tabar, Linda. "From Third World Internationalism to 'The Internationals': The Transformation of Solidarity with Palestine," *Third World Quarterly* 38.2 (2017): 414-35.

Tamari, Salim. "The Future of Jerusalem: Sacred Space or Open City," *Institute for Palestine Studies*, 11 July 2011, <http://www.palestine-studies.org/institute/fellows/future-jerusalem-sacred-space-or-open-city>. Accessed 28 February 2017.

Taraki, Lisa. "Even-Handedness and the Palestinian-Israeli/Israeli-Palestinian "Conflict."" *Contemporary Sociology* 35.5 (Sept 2006): 449-53.

Thrall, Nathan. "How the West Chose War in Gaza." *New York Times* 17 July 2014: A23.

"Through Women's Eyes: A PCHR Report on the Gender-Specific Impact and Consequences of Operation Cast Lead," *Palestine Centre for Human Rights*, 28 September 2009, <https://pchrgaza.org/en/?p=4738>. Accessed 15 July 2016.

Turner, Mandy. "The Political Economy of Western Aid." *Decolonizing Palestinian Political Economy*. Eds Mandy Turner and Omar Shweiki. Hampshire: Palgrave, 2014. 32-52.

United Nations Commission on Human Rights. "*Civil and Political Rights, Including the Questions of: Torture and Detention.*" E/CN.4/2002/NGO/162 (20 February 2002), available from <https://unispal.un.org/DPA/DPR/unispal.nsf/0/E5DFDA7A80736EC185256B89005BC22C>.

United Nations Environment Program. "*Environmental Assessment of the Gaza Strip.*" (September 2009). <https://unispal.un.org/pdfs/DEP_1190_GE.pdf>.

United Nations, General Assembly. "Importance of the Universal Realization of the Right of Peoples to Self Determination and of the Speedy Granting of Independence to Colonial Countries and Peoples for the Effective Guarantee and Observance of Human Rights," A/RES/3246 (29 November 1974), available from <https://unispal.un.org/DPA/DPR/unispal.nsf/0/C867EE1DBF29A6E5852568C6006B2F0C>. Accessed 30 March 2017.

—. *Situation of Human Rights in the Palestinian Territories Occupied Since 1967.* A/65/331 (30 August 2010) 17, available from <https://unispal.un.org/

DPA/DPR/unispal.nsf/eed216406b50bf6485256ce10072f637/
69bec99af727eac2852577c3004aad8a? OpenDocument>. Accessed
4 August 2016.

—. "Special Committee Calls for Security Council Sanctions Against
Israel for 'Culture of Impunity' Regarding Arab Rights in Occupied
Lands," GA/SPD/361 (6 November 2006), available from <http://
www.un.org/press/en/2006/gaspd361.doc.htm>. Accessed 13
February 2017.

United Nations Human Rights Council. *Report of the Detailed Findings
of the Independent Commission of Inquiry Established Pursuant to
Human Rights Council Resolution S-21/1*, A/HRC/29/52 (22 June
2015), available from <http://www.ohchr.org/EN/HRBodies/
HRC/CoIGazaConflict/Pages/ReportCoIGaza.aspx#report>.
Accessed 15 February 2017.

United Nations Human Rights Council, *Report of the United Nations
High Commissioner for Human Rights on the implementation of
Human Rights Council resolutions S-9/1 and S-12/*, A/HRC/22/35 (6
March 2013), available from <http://www.ohchr.org/Documents/
HRBodies/HRCouncil/RegularSession/Session22/A.HRC.22.35_
AUV.pdf>. Accessed 13 February 2017.

—. *"Report of the Special Rapporteur on the Situation of Human Rights
in the Palestinian Territories Occupied Since 1967, John Dugard."*
A/HRC/4/17 (29 January 2007), available from < https://
documents-dds-ny.un.org/doc/UNDOC/GEN/G07/105/44/PDF/
G0710544.pdf?OpenElement>. Accessed 26 July 2016.

United Nations Office for the Coordination of Humanitarian Affairs
Occupied Palestinian Territories. *"The Humanitarian Impact of
Gaza's Electricity and Fuel Crisis."* (March 2014), available from
<https://www.ochaopt.org/documents/ocha_opt_electricity_
factsheet_march_2014_english.pdf >. Accessed 26 July 2016

—. *West Bank Movement and Access Update*. (May 2009), available from <https://unispal.un.org/DPA/DPR/UNISPAL.NSF/9a798adbf32 2 a f f 3 8 5 2 5 6 1 7 b 0 0 6 d 8 8 d 7 / b 3 e d b b 7 6 d a f d d d 6a852575c20065e305?OpenDocument>. Accessed 9 August 2016.

United Nations Relief and Works Agency. The United Nations Country Team (UNCT) in the Occupied Palestinian Territory (oPt). "*Gaza in 2020: A Livable Place?*" August 2012. 16 www.unrwa.org/ userfiles/file/publications/gaza/Gaza%20in%202020.pdf. Accessed 5 July 2016.

United Nations Relief and Works Agency. "*OPT Emergency Appeal Report 2013*." (30 April 2014) <https://www.unrwa.org/resources/ reports/opt-emergency-appeal-report-2013>. Accessed 25 February 2017.

Uscinski, Joseph. *The People's News*. New York: NYU P, 2014.

"Wanted Militant Dies in Gaza Raid," *BBC*, 8 June 2006, <http://news.bbc. co.uk/2/hi/middle_east/5062360.stm>. Accessed 13 October 2016.

"Water for One People Only," *Al-Haq*, 2013. <http://www.alhaq.org/ publications/Water-For-One-People-Only.pdf>.

"Yasser Arafat: From Beyond the Grave," editorial, *The Guardian*, 8 November 2013: GRDN 34.

ACKNOWLEDGMENTS

Thanks to Bhaskar Sunkara for helping make this book happen. Max Ajl has my endless gratitude for reading an early draft of the book and providing invaluable feedback, as do all of the other profound thinkers, committed organizers, and generous souls who read the book and offered an endorsement. I am deeply in debt to all of the extraordinary intellectuals and activists working toward a just resolution to the question of Palestine whose work is referenced in these pages; my admiration and respect for everyone struggling for that goal is boundless irrespective of whether they have directly shaped this book. Thanks to my brilliant wife, Karen O'Keefe, for the unremitting support. I have also immeasurably profited from the lifelong love and friendship of my parents, my siblings, my late grandparents, and my pets. An enthusiastic note of gratitude to everyone at OR Books who worked on this project is also in order.

www.ingramcontent.com/pod-product-compliance
Lightning Source LLC
Jackson TN
JSHW081329130125
77033JS00014B/472

* 9 7 8 1 6 8 2 1 9 1 2 8 6 *